Managing Training and Development in Museums:
A Guide

Elaine Kilgour and Brian Martin

SCOTTISH
MUSEUMS
COUNCIL

EDINBURGH: THE STATIONERY OFFICE

© Scottish Museums Council 1997

First published 1997 by
The Stationery Office Ltd
21 South Gyle Crescent, Edinburgh EH12 9EB

Application for reproduction should be made to: The Stationery Office Ltd
21 South Gyle Crescent, Edinburgh EH12 9EB

British Library Cataloguing in Publication Data

A catalogue record for this book is available from the British Library

ISBN 0 11 495853 X

The National Occupational Standards for Museums and Heritage were
developed with Crown funding.
This material is Crown copyright and is reproduced under licence from the
Controller of Her Majesty's Stationery Office.

Contents

About the Authors

Elaine Kilgour is Training Manager with the Scottish Museums Council. Her responsibilities include planning, organising and managing the Council's training service, developing standards-based training materials and providing advocacy and advice on training and development in museums. She has advised on a number of training packages and publications and is a sector group member of the Scottish Qualifications Authority.

Brian Martin is currently Senior Lecturer in the Department of Arts & Humanities of Moray House Institute, Edinburgh and Director of the Institute's Unit for the Study of Cultural Administration. His professional interests in museums include not only management training, but also the development of museum education. He is currently co-director of an EU Socrates project on adult education and museum partnerships.

The Scottish Museums Council

The Scottish Museums Council is an independent company principally funded by the Secretary of State for Scotland. The Council's mission is to improve the quality of museum and gallery provision in Scotland. This it seeks to do by providing a wide range of advice, services and financial assistance to its membership, and by representing the interests of museums in Scotland.

The Arts Management Training Initiative – Scotland (AMTIS)

The Arts Management Training Initiative – Scotland was a partnership involving the national cultural agencies and other bodies with a strategic interest in Scotland's cultural sector, established in 1991 to develop management training for the sector.

WEB Associates

WEB Associates (Richard Ellis, Sinclair Broomfield and the late Dr Sara Whiteley) are consultants specialising in training needs analysis and communication audits in both the public and private sectors. WEB undertook the developmental work in relation to training needs analysis in Scottish museums, with AMTIS and on behalf of the Scottish Museums Council. They also collaborated in the production of this book.

All involved in its production regret the untimely death of Dr Sarah Whiteley and would like to pay tribute to her for the enthusiasm and professionalism she brought to the project.

Foreword

by Mr Sam Galbraith MP
Scottish Office Minister with responsibility for the Arts

Museums play an active role in our culture and society. Improvement and progress in the quality of service which they provide to their visitors depends on developing the individuals who work in them – both paid and voluntary alike – to make an effective contribution. By investing in training and development for their staff, museum managers can enable positive change to flourish.

As learning organisations, museums are perhaps uniquely placed to promote lifelong learning, but first of all they must create such a climate for their staff. This publication provides practical advice and help on where to place the staff training and development issue within museums. I welcome and commend it to you.

Acknowledgements

Managing Training and Development in Museums: A Guide is the product of collaboration among a large number of individuals and institutions whose advice and comments were invaluable.

We would like to record our thanks to all of those who took part in the training needs analyses which contributed to the research process used to inform the production of this book. We would like to thank in particular Timothy Ambrose, formerly Director of the Scottish Museums Council, whose commitment to and support of training and development provided encouragement to transform a proposal into a working project.

Thanks are also due to all at WEB Associates; James Blair, Perth and Kinross Council; Dallas Mechan, Fife Council; Colin McLean, formerly of the Scottish Mining Museum; Moira Mackenzie, Helmsdale Heritage Society; Owen Mullen, Summerlee Industrial Museum; Kris Bachoo, formerly of Glasgow Museums and Art Galleries; Herbert Coutts and Derek Janes, City of Edinburgh Council; Margaret Greeves, Fitzwilliam Museum, Cambridge; Elizabeth Baker, Training Officer, Area Museum Council for the South-West; and all whose critical evaluation has contributed to the refinement of these materials.

Finally, to Dave Aikman and Aileen Robertson, Moray House Design Studio, our thanks for their assistance with the design and format of this book, and to all of our colleagues for their support throughout.

Elaine Kilgour
Training Manager
Scottish Museums Council

Brian Martin
Senior Lecturer
Department of Arts and
Humanities
Moray House Institute

1. Introduction

This book was commissioned by the Scottish Museums Council and prepared with the assistance of the Arts Management Training Initiative – Scotland and WEB Associates. In developing a self-help approach, the Council's objective is to enable museums to explore the stages through which they need to pass in order to achieve the basis for the systematic and continuous development of a confident and skilled workforce.

A Training Needs Analysis (TNA) allows museums to make informed choices about the best and most appropriate style of training and development for their own staff. But the TNA process must be fully integrated into the forward planning process of the museum as a whole. Only if training and development are seen as an integral part of a museum's long-term planning will existing skills and competencies, and those acquired as part of a systematic development process, combine to make the basis of effective contribution. Managing the training function must become as important as managing collections and visitor services.

> The success of your museum will ultimately depend not on your users, or on your displays, but on the skills and abilities of those working for the museum.
>
> Ambrose, 1993

> The quality of service a museum provides depends heavily on having a highly committed, well managed, informed, skilled and effective workforce. Training is essential for the development of this resource and in helping museums meet their identified organisational objectives. Thus, it is an important investment for all museums.
>
> Scottish Museums Council Training and Development Policy Statement, 1992

This book aims to provide advice to museums of all sizes and types on the subject of training and staff development. It will not only show you how to look at the museum, team, and individual training needs – in other words, a TNA – but also where and when it is appropriate to place and consider the whole staff development issue in museums.

Whenever the term 'staff' is used, this is understood to mean anyone working in a museum, whether they be professional or technical, paid or unpaid, full-time or part-time and in any area of

museum work. This necessarily includes committee members and trustees.

The term 'museum' will be used throughout to include art galleries. Also, although it is entitled *Managing Training and Development in Museums: A Guide*, the term 'training' is used advisedly and should be taken to mean staff development in the broadest sense.

It is not just about sending people away on training courses, but about offering people the opportunity to broaden their knowledge, skills and attitudes through a variety of channels both within and outwith their place of work. The introduction of Continuing Professional Development (CPD) as a requirement for new applicants for Associate Membership of the Museums Association (AMA) has increased pressure for a move away from 'training' in its traditional sense to a much wider interpretation of 'learning'.

Getting Started

This book is designed to allow you to choose where to begin. It is recommended that you do not attempt to read it all at once although, of course, this is possible especially if you wish to remodel completely the whole approach which your museum takes to staff development and training issues. However, a better approach would be to browse through the contents, first noting which sections are of immediate relevance and interest to the situation in your museum. You can then work your way through these gradually.

For example, you could use it to identify and try out a new approach:

- to the identification of the training needs of staff;
- to assess the effectiveness of the techniques which are currently in use; or
- to check what progress has been made to date to prepare and implement a staff development strategy.

In some chapters, you will find a variety of activities to work through and these will be indicated in the text by an activity icon. The Tool Kit contains sample forms, questionnaires etc. which you can photocopy and use to carry out a TNA, together with guidance on how to draft job descriptions, person specifications, action plans etc. The format of the book has been designed to encourage you to gather and keep all of the necessary supporting papers together.

Chapter 4 contains a checklist in the form of a flowchart (pp. 22-23) against which you can review the situation in your museum. Ideally, you should work your way through the flowchart and refer to the appropriate chapters which will show you how to prepare and put together all the different elements of a strategy to develop a systematic approach to TNA in your museum.

You can, of course, get started on a TNA right away if you wish. Nevertheless, if you do not think about having the required elements in place before you look at training needs, you will find it more difficult to see what to do with the information you gather and how individual staff training needs fit into what you would like your museum to achieve.

If you work in a small museum and this process seems a little daunting, turn to p. 35 where you will find an alternative approach to tackling your training and development planning.

Regardless of the approach you take, this book offers you the possibility to promote coherent and, most importantly, useful training and development opportunities within your museum.

> **Future success will depend on the best possible use of people, collections and finances. Without a proper staff development strategy this cannot and will not happen. A sustainable staff development strategy is in turn dependent on effective analysis of current and future training and development needs.**

2. Training, Development and the Museum Environment

This book is not about training as such, nor is it an analysis of the changing relationships between museums, community and society. However, it is worth reviewing some of these themes briefly in order that the function of a TNA is seen in a holistic context. It is also relevant to clarify some terms at the outset.

Training and Development

'**Training**' can be described as a process concerned with the acquisition or maintenance of capability. The word 'capability' is important here. Arguably it is only through training that an employee becomes able to do a job efficiently by acquiring the necessary knowledge and skills in a systematic and organised way.

While there is much 'learning on the job' evident in museums, and while museum curators and managers are increasingly aware of the importance of training and likely to send staff on courses, decisions are often made casually as to which course is selected and who goes on what. It also appears to be the case that there is little systematic attention given to disseminating information gathered by attendance at courses and seminars, or 'cascading' the benefits of training workshops and courses to other staff members.

However, it is becoming more widely accepted that staff require more focused and better co-ordinated training and development opportunities. Training should also be regarded as an ongoing process; it should not be reserved, for example, only for the purpose of **induction**.

> I've really received no training other than basic knowledge of how things work in the office.
>
> Clerical assistant

> Attendants feel particularly neglected. Very few staff could remember having received training of any sort. Some had been on a Local Authority induction course, but find this inapplicable to their working environment.
>
> Consultant's report

The concept of '**development**' is less clear than that of training. The Institute of Training and Development has defined human resource development as being 'that process whereby people develop their full potential in life and work'. Training and development can thus be regarded as integrated.

This concept of **integration** and the related theme of **continuity** is emphasised in much contemporary management theory about training and development. This sees development of the person in, and through, the job as an increasingly important aspect of job satisfaction.

Continuing Professional Development (CPD) places emphasis on individuals maintaining and developing their professional competence throughout their careers. In other sectors, the integration of individual and organisational development through the encouragement or facilitation of training and development has seen the growth of the '**learning organisation**'.

Whether focused on the individual or organisational level, however, it is commonly accepted that programmes of training and development should be concentrated on identifying and achieving a realisation of needs. There are thus a number of reasons why **training needs** should be the focus of any systematic attempt to plan training and development provision within a museum.

One view is that TNA should be focused on the 'skills gap' which occurs when the knowledge and skills of a member of staff are insufficient to do a job properly. This may be caused by change within the job itself or within the organisation as a whole. In each of these instances, there is a need for training in order to bring employees up to the required standard and to equip them to do the tasks for which they are employed.

In all of these cases, there is a need for a **systematic** and **strategic** approach to the identification of training needs. The contemporary literature on human resource management theory is consistent in the belief that this is essential to realise the **potential of training** as a tool of **individual and organisational development in the museum** itself.

Taking a **strategic approach** formalises the identification of needs by providing a step-by-step guide as to: what needs are; how they are going to be met; the time-scales involved; and the outcomes achieved. Thus, needs are identified, but the **process** of meeting the need is also addressed as well as the choices of training strategy. There are clear steps that can be adopted in this process and these are outlined in Chapter 8.

Underlying these steps, there should be a **belief** that training should not be seen as an isolated function but as part of the **overall development strategy** of the organisation itself.

The benefits of training and development approached in this way are tangible. They can also be defined as '**intrinsic**' and '**extrinsic**'. Examples of 'intrinsic' benefits for the individual are, for example, improved performance or increased motivation, whilst examples of 'extrinsic' benefits include opportunities for promotion.

The overall benefit for the museum itself, however, can be stated as a greater opportunity to achieve organisational goals such as the successful transition from provisional to full Registration, enhanced collections care, improved visitor satisfaction, increased revenue from retail operations etc.

Perceptions of this sort have been to the fore in Scottish Museums Council thinking for some time. In *Forward Planning: A Handbook of Business, Corporate and Development Planning for Museums and Galleries* (1991), Ambrose set out the benefits of addressing training as a key feature of strategic development and planning as a cyclical process.

identify training needs > enhance skills > improve quality of service > increase job satisfaction >

The Museum and its Environment

It is commonplace when discussing the nature and role of museums in contemporary society and when considering their potential contribution, to be able to list multiple and often apparently competing priorities at a time when resources are either becoming more scarce or having to be stretched further.

This is the case regardless of size, and affects small museums reliant on volunteers and community support every bit as much as established local authority museums or the large national institutions.

It has been argued that the museum profession is in the process of re-formation and that this process will create new and different museum professionals and museum institutions. It is clear that museum professionals themselves feel the growing pressures of change and a growing need to address change pro-actively. In such a process, **training and development** are agreed as having a fundamental role to play.

> My training was adequate at the time because most of us training to be guides already had good communication skills. However, the remit of the museum is changing and this will mean new training is required.
>
> Volunteer

This is also the case in thinking about the place of the museum in the market place. Against a trend of increasing attendances at museums, museums still appear to be an under-utilised asset and only 25% of museums reached their full capacity on even one day during the year (MTI Workforce Survey, 1993). Some evidence points to the possibility that museum attendances may have reached a natural limit, which, taken with increasing competition from a widening range of leisure providers may present demands for additional knowledge, understanding and skills requirements amongst museum workers.

The pressure that this creates appears to be one of many with training implications. A 1993 pilot study for the Museum Training Institute (Kahn and Garden, 1993) examining job attitudes, sources of job dissatisfaction, and potential job stress among museum employees and the relation these have to training issues, determined that people working in museums have increasing concerns about their working environment, work patterns, the management of their organisation, job prospects and training.

Amongst the major concerns identified in the course of the study were:

Management style
- lack of human resource development and training skills amongst directors and middle managers;
- lack of objective setting and autonomy for middle managers;
- lack of consultation and feedback.

Job definition/extension
- poor documentation resources;
- conflicting tasks and demands in the job.

Organisational structure
- sales and marketing not recognised as a primary function;
- managing volunteers and casual labour at expense of other work;
- exposure of individuals to negative feedback from the public.

Narrow skill base
- lack of pre-museum work experience and training;
- lack of training in technical subjects for women.

Other issues
- poor time management skills and inadequate understanding of managerial role;
- demotivation caused by perceived low status of museum.

The report concluded that, if not addressed, these concerns have the potential to result in decreased efficiency in museums and reduced motivation, increased job dissatisfaction and occupational stress amongst museum employees.

This concern was also noted by the Museum Training Institute in 1993, when it calculated that the average spend in the museum sector in Britain on training was just over 1% of total staff costs – half that recommended by the Hale Report of 1987 (Museums & Galleries Commission, 1987) which noted for example,

> . . . little investment in management training despite the fact that the most noticeable characteristic of the museum and gallery world is its rate of growth and its increasing diversity.

The increasing range of roles museums are called upon to play as agents of economic development through tourism; of community development and social regeneration; and of education, personal growth and development is well documented. Other increasing pressures within the external environment such as:

- political change at all levels;
- changing public tastes and expectations;
- impact of media technology;
- the emergence of a multi-cultural society with attendant pluralistic values and equal opportunities imperatives

are also familiar to museum professionals.

These pressures are coupled with demands for income-generation. They are also linked to diversification and expansion of the range of services to include catering, retailing and merchandising related to changes in patterns of usage of museums by the public and standstill budgets in many publicly funded museums. Taken together, these factors present a powerful range of stimulants to creative thinking on the use of the 'human resource asset' or the **people available to the museum**.

This can present a powerful opportunity to look critically at the area of training and development in the museum and use it as a catalyst to **taking charge of the process of change**.

Yet in a sector where 45% of professionals expect to remain in their current position and 25% to be promoted within their current organisations, it is of concern that only one third of museums have a training plan or dedicated training budget. In many cases, these stop short of being fully comprehensive by exclusively focusing on curatorial staff training, or by ignoring the training needs and aspirations of volunteers, for example.

> *A*ll I know is that you are more likely to get on a course at the end of the financial year than in the middle.
>
> Assistant Keeper

> Well, we don't have a training plan as such, but I can give you a list of the courses that people have attended recently.
>
> Curator

Thus there can be seen to be many justifications as to why **TNA** is a key concept in respect of museum development.

Assessing the Current Position

In January 1994, AMTIS (the Arts Management Training Initiative – Scotland) was commissioned by the Scottish Museums Council to begin a programme of work which would enhance museums' capacities to develop the framework for a coherent and systematic approach to TNA in museums.

The impetus for this came from the introduction of Scottish/National Vocational Qualifications for the museums, galleries and heritage sector. This national initiative has created the opportunity for museums to introduce a cost-effective and measurable system which provides a structure for both staff development and museum development – a structure which is also flexible and adaptable enough to be used in different types of institution.

Similarly, the development of **Investors in People** as the national standard which enables organisations to improve their performance through the effective training and development of all their people to meet the organisation's objectives provides an additional opportunity for museums to improve the way they both organise and manage the training and development of their staff.

Working with WEB Associates, AMTIS undertook a series of 'case study' TNAs of selected museums in membership of the Scottish Museums Council. These museums varied in size, type and location. The group included:

- a small rural museum heavily reliant on volunteers;
- a medium-sized local authority museum service;
- a working industrial museum;
- a social and industrial heritage museum;
- a small local authority museum service.

The case studies were undertaken with two main aims in mind:

- to pilot, trial and test instruments and techniques which might be of use in self-help TNA;
- to consider the practicalities of undertaking TNA in museums.

The willing involvement of the curators, staff and volunteers of the case study museums is acknowledged elsewhere and the 'lessons' of the case studies are used throughout this publication.

In summary, what was found in the case studies was evidence of considerable concern for, and recognition of, the importance of training. Much was happening of a positive nature. For example:

- more care was being taken with regard to selection of courses for staff to attend;
- more staff were obtaining access to training;
- imaginative and low cost approaches to options other than conventional courses were being adopted, e.g. skill exchanges with other museums; securing (free) access to courses run in-house by large companies in the locality.

However, managers of the case study museums (all of which had in their different ways thought long and hard about training) felt there was still room for improvement in their approach. It is perhaps natural that this should be the case, given the pace of change and the pressures on and within museums as outlined above.

In 1993, 64.5% of UK museums were reported in the Museum Training Institute's Workforce Survey as having no training plan (50.9% of local authority museums). 75.7% of museums admitted they had undertaken no skills audit or TNA (72.2% of local authority museums).

Most, if not all, museums currently undertake training and development for their staff. Some of this is done 'on the job' or by attending short sessions or studying for further professional qualifications, and the range of training activities under this heading is very wide.

The need for this training will probably have been identified on a relatively ad hoc basis with the museum responding to changing demands or seeking to develop some staff to meet new roles, for example, in Visitor Services. Alternatively, it may have been identified through staff appraisal, career review schemes or a new staff member who wishes to continue development in a relevant professional area of work.

> In $2\frac{1}{2}$ years, I've only had 15 minutes group instruction on using the computerised till.
>
> Museum Assistant

> I circulate the brochures that we receive on training courses and see who wants to go on what one – it's usually a question of first come, first served.
>
> Curator

Thus a number of sources may have been used to identify needs including:

- national developments in museum use and management;
- visitor feedback;
- experience of the introduction of new systems, e.g. information technology;
- requests from individuals or small groups of staff;
- job descriptions and person specifications;
- appraisal or career review schemes;
- interviews with staff on particular performance issues;
- role analysis and review by managers dealing with changing demands.

What is often missing, however, is a **systematic** and **comprehensive** approach to identifying training needs for the whole organisation.

This is why undertaking a TNA can be a very valuable **management tool** for determining at a given point what the needs are, conceptualising common and individual skills and knowledge required and helping to develop plans to meet the needs in a systematic and cost-effective way.

The principal objective underlying the production of this book is, therefore, to help change the prevailing situation and provide museums with a firm foundation for planning and developing, implementing and evaluating training with a view to enhancing staff performance, job satisfaction and the status of the museum itself.

The key question is, therefore, how can the training needs of staff and the organisation best be identified?

What is Training Needs Analysis (TNA)?

Essentially, TNA is a process for defining the 'gap' between what the current position is in relation to organisational and staff performance at work and what this should be – or what will be needed in the foreseeable future. It identifies the gaps in knowledge, skill and attitudes and seeks to identify, through museum-wide personal development plans, the most cost-effective way to meet those needs.

The model below provides a summary of the key points:

Current Position	What It Should Be
• Organisational performance	• What the museum should be achieving now or in the immediate future – standards/targets
• Knowledge, skills and attitudes currently held	• Knowledge skills and attitudes required
• Actual performance of individuals	• Required performance in terms of standards and targets

Thus, TNA can be looked at in terms of **gaps**.

Present situation

Job we do . . . present skills . . . actual performance . . . potential gap.

Future

Jobs we may be doing . . . future skills . . . future performance . . . likely gap.

Using this approach, training needs can be analysed for:

- the **museum** as a **whole**;
- a **department**, **section**, **function** or **occupation group**;
- **individual members of staff** or **volunteers**.

This book assumes that a museum-wide TNA is to be undertaken, although the principles and approach can be applied to elements of the organisation. The value in identifying collective needs is that they can often be met in a more cost-effective way, and can help the manager to plan and finance training over a reasonable time-scale.

What is the Overall Approach Needed to Undertake a TNA?

In a comprehensive TNA, a wide range of information sources within the museum together with significant external sources of influence are examined to provide the means for identifying the 'gap'. These are addressed in more detail later in the book but in summary in a large museum they might include:

Whole museum level of analysis

- senior managers' perceptions of the developments facing the museum over the next 3 to 5 years;
- the views of Trustees and funding bodies;
- national developments affecting museums;
- visitor surveys;
- national standards and targets of performance.

Department, functional or occupational level of analysis

- departmental assessment of needs by managers and supervisors of staff;
- specific demands on a department or occupational group to changes in role;
- specific occupational/professional group needs;
- visitor feedback about the performance of a particular department;
- new technological developments impacting on a particular group;
- current training budgets, activities and plans at departmental level.

Individual level of analysis

- job descriptions (statements about the duties, tasks, responsibilities, and/or key activities of the job holder);
- person specifications (analysis of the knowledge, skills and attitudes required for competent performance in the job);
- staff development/appraisal/career review information;
- individual training/development plans;
- individual perceptions about training/developments needs;
- assessment of individual performance with particular reference to performance gaps in the areas of knowledge, skills and/or attitudes.

Summary

The methods used in a TNA are therefore aimed at gathering and analysing information from these and other sources, and providing a systematic presentation of the training and development needs of individuals, teams and the museum as a whole. From this, proposals and plans as to the most appropriate ways to meet needs can be developed, taking account of local needs and circumstances. The TNA is an important method of enhancing the effectiveness of the museum in meeting its strategic objectives.

The approach suggested and most of the techniques and tools highlighted in this book are designed to be applicable to museums of all sizes and types. Regardless of the number of people working in the museum on a paid or voluntary basis, the type of systematic approach recommended should be of benefit to them, to you and to the museum as a whole. However, it is recognised that small museums and museums which employ a lot of volunteers can have particular requirements. Therefore, these situations are discussed in Chapter 4.

3. Managing Training in Museums

> A museum is an institution which collects, documents, preserves, exhibits and interprets material evidence and associated information for the public benefit.
>
> The Museums Association's definition of a museum

But where do people fit into this? The museum 'institution' referred to above is not an abstract idea but is made up of the people who have worked there in the past, who work there now, and those who will be recruited to work there in the future. But how well do museums – which are dedicated to the collection and care of **objects** – look after the **people** whose job it is to carry out this function?

> I applied to go on a course recently – it was just what I needed at this stage in my career – but permission was refused. I don't really know why.
>
> Conservation Officer

When an object is donated to, or purchased for, a museum it brings its own 'story' with it. It receives a unique number and is formally accessioned into the collection. Its conservation and storage needs are assessed; it may be developed through display and interpretation. Contrast this treatment with that of the new museum assistant or volunteer who joins the staff. Both bring their own unique experience and knowledge. But how are their needs catered for? How are they developed? And why should each be treated in isolation?

The quality of service which a museum provides depends heavily on having a highly committed, well managed, informed, skilled and effective workforce. Training is essential for the development of this 'resource' and in helping museums meet their identified objectives. It is an important investment for all museums, but it is sometimes regarded as an expensive cost.

Training should be regarded as an integral part of the overall improvement and development of the museum itself. It has a strategic contribution to make to the museum because the museum will not achieve what it wants to if it does not have a sufficient number of people with the required skills and knowledge to put this into effect.

It's not just about courses but team involvement aiming to break down gaps that exist between the various levels – team building if you like, together with personal development and job enrichment.

Curator

Museums seek to create a 'learning environment' for their visitors, but it is also necessary to consider how they can create a learning environment within the museum, so that staff get used to developing themselves and learning from each other. For example, the practice of asking staff who have been on a course to report back to colleagues is not as common as one might think.

This reporting back via short informal presentations and/or brief written reports not only enables others to share ideas, but creates an expectation that training is not entirely about individual self-fulfilment – team and museum development becomes a recognised goal as well.

Clearly, museum managers have a key role to play in this and they have a fundamental responsibility for the training and development of their staff. They can influence the whole attitude within the museum by creating and maintaining a positive outlook on training, by identifying and arguing for funding for training, and by being an example through their own participation and commitment.

It does not follow, however, that the senior manager has to have responsibility for managing the training function within museums. This can be delegated to any person with appropriate knowledge, understanding and skills and a designated staff development responsibility. It does not necessarily have to be an extra member of staff, although in large museum services, a dedicated post may be a more realistic option. This individual is not responsible for making all decisions about who receives what training, but he/she manages the training function within the museum by making sure that everyone has the opportunity of being offered training, gets access to training and provides feedback from it.

Regardless of whoever is assigned the responsibility, this should be clearly indicated in that individual's job description. It is essential that he/she is given not only the time and resources necessary to carry out this function but also the support and commitment of the museum's management. Without this, it will be very difficult for any individual to promote change or introduce a different approach and actually carry it through.

In a Local Authority context, it is vital that this individual builds a good working relationship with the central personnel/training unit. In a large museum service, it is important that this person should work closely with the internal personnel function of the museum (if the two functions are divorced). In small independent museums, the development, maintenance and collaborative use of volunteers may be a key task for the sole paid employee or for volunteers themselves where there is no paid employee. In each case, the training function is equally important, though it may be 'managed' differently.

Regardless of the type and size of the museum, a checklist of what the person responsible for the training and staff development function should do is the same. An overview of this is contained in the checklist in Chapter 4, but essentially this person must:

- have an overview of all staff training needs within the museum, to ensure that a museum-wide view can be taken of what is happening and that there is a balance between individual needs and museum needs;
- have responsibility for managing and dispersing the training budget;
- evaluate how effective the training activity has been;
- ensure that records are kept of training activities.

Increasingly, it is apparent that many museums regard training as a part of wider staff development. This is demonstrated by the existence of staff development interviews, appraisals and career planning. Here, aspects such as mapping out key results areas can prove useful in providing staff with a clearer focus as to their main duties. This also assists in the conduct of appraisals systems since clearly defined areas can be targeted.

There is a need, however, to see training as much more than attending a course, or gaining qualifications. It is also, for example, about coaching and mentoring, shadowing a colleague, or being seconded to another section, perhaps even another museum.

> Museums tend to be parochial – there's no real collaboration. I'd like to see more co-operation involving museums; there's a lot to be learnt from each other.
>
> Volunteer

Training defined comprehensively enables people in museums to:

- develop new skills, e.g. by acquiring a new display technique;
- increase knowledge, e.g. through research on a geological specimen;
- keep abreast of new developments, e.g. by reading about a new conservation technique;
- review and reflect on current practice, e.g. by introducing a new management concept;
- improve effectiveness, e.g. by tying their education service more closely to the schools' curricula;
- meet their museum's changing needs, e.g. by developing the range of stock available in the museum shop;
- address changing needs and aspirations of visitors, e.g. for more effective interpretation.

In these examples of how people in museums can benefit from training, it is important to note that all of them could be achieved by a different training approach or method. For example, staff can develop a new display technique by speaking to a designer from another museum. They can read and keep up with new developments or they can visit other museums which demonstrate good practice, learn how they do things, and assess their own practice against this – an approach sometimes referred to as 'benchmarking'.

More traditionally, they could attend a short course to develop their management style. They could spend a morning with a member of the advisory staff from an Area Museum Council or the museum's curatorial advisor – all of these approaches involve development in its fullest sense, and they all develop both the staff member *and* the museum service.

Since the publication of the Hale Report on Museum Training (Museums & Galleries Commission, 1987), training has been increasingly recognised to be of vital importance to museums. Significant national changes have taken place, including the creation of the Museum Training Institute in 1989. Workplace-based Scottish/National Vocational Qualifications (S/NVQs) are available for all aspects of museum work and at all levels. Continuing Professional Development (CPD) is a requirement for the achievement of the Associate Membership of the Museums Association (AMA), and the development of a training policy has been identified as being of benefit to museums registering under the Museums & Galleries Commission Registration Scheme. The range of training options available to museums is growing but how many are in a position to accept this challenge?

What were the lessons learned from the case studies developed in this book?

Museums should be encouraged to give high priority to their staff development needs and to allocate sufficient funding and time so that all categories of staff can receive appropriate training.

Job descriptions (where they exist) have in the past become frozen; in some cases there has been too little matching between the description and the actual job done. It is important that job descriptions are regularly reviewed to take account of the effects of external changes on the museum and its response to these opportunities and threats. Such reviews need to be linked to forward planning so that the staffing structure not only mirrors past needs but also anticipates future trends and developments.

Where applicable, museums should consider developing a range of in-house training initiatives and, wherever possible, co-operative programmes with other museums, through museums fora, interest groups, etc.

Greater attention should be given to monitoring and evaluating training. Identifying training needs and participating in a training and development activity are only parts of the equation – it is also essential to evaluate whether or not that activity makes or has made a difference. This evaluation must be built into the process when the activity is being planned – not bolted on after the event as an afterthought. Suggested formats for a pre-training activity questionnaire and a post-training activity questionnaire are included in the Tool Kit on (pp. 128-131).

It is increasingly important for museums to draw up a training strategy and training plans for all staff members. Some have responded very well to staff requests for training: however, this has tended to be on an ad hoc basis whereby senior staff have responded to individual requests.

Ad hoc training has been supplemented in some cases by more planned approaches to professional development, on behalf of keepers and curators and, occasionally, attendants. Increasingly however, it is vital that all staff are encouraged to think of training not just as an ad hoc activity, but as a way of moving the museum forward to meeting new opportunities and succeeding against threats and competitors.

In this sense, planning and developing training should be seen as an integral part of strategic thinking and forward planning – a point which will be developed in Chapter 8.

Activity

It may be worth reviewing some of the influences on training and development in your museum before considering how best to develop and manage effective training related to a systematic assessment of needs.

List the five most dominant external and internal pressures on your museum and work through the following questions.

External Pressures

1.

2.

3.

4.

5.

Internal Pressures

1.

2.

3.

4.

5.

What are the training and development implications arising from each of these?

Do you have a training and development plan or strategy which addresses these implications?

Yes   No

If not, see checklist (pp. 21-34.)

If you do, how would you rate the plan on a scale of 1 to 10 in terms of its capacity to use training to deal with the pressures identified?

What is your museum's current mission?
Please list up to five objectives.

1.

2.

3.

4.

5.

To what extent does your training and development plan help you to realise these? Rate your plan on a scale of 1 to 10.

What are the weaknesses of the plan in respect of pressures on your museum at present and your key aims?

Using a scale of 1 to 10, assess the extent to which your plan or strategy is based on an objective and comprehensive analysis of training needs.

4. Checklist Before You Start

This chapter considers all the components of a comprehensive staff development strategy. These have been represented on the next page as a checklist. Work your way through these gradually.

It is recommended that you set aside a ring-binder(s) – or box file(s) – in which you can store details of all these components. You may not have many of them in place yet, but you can still use the checklist to work your way through the steps involved at the pace most appropriate to your museum.

Once you have compiled your training and development ring-binder(s) you should have together in one place all the documentation needed to manage your training and development effectively.

If you have a commitment to staff training and development, read on.

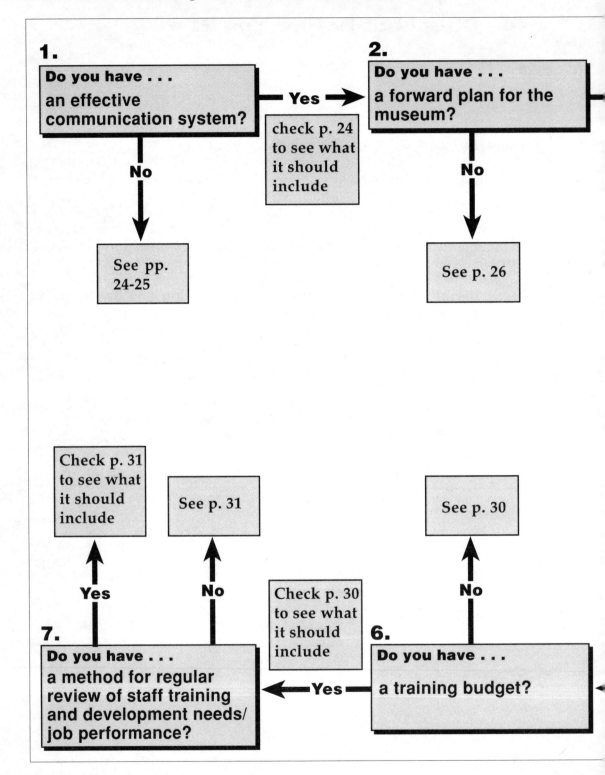

1.

Do you have . . .

an effective communication system?

Yes → check p. 24 to see what it should include

No

See pp. 24-25

2.

Do you have . . .

a forward plan for the museum?

No

See p. 26

Check p. 31 to see what it should include

See p. 31

See p. 30

Yes

No

Check p. 30 to see what it should include

No

7.

Do you have . . .

a method for regular review of staff training and development needs/ job performance?

← Yes —

6.

Do you have . . .

a training budget?

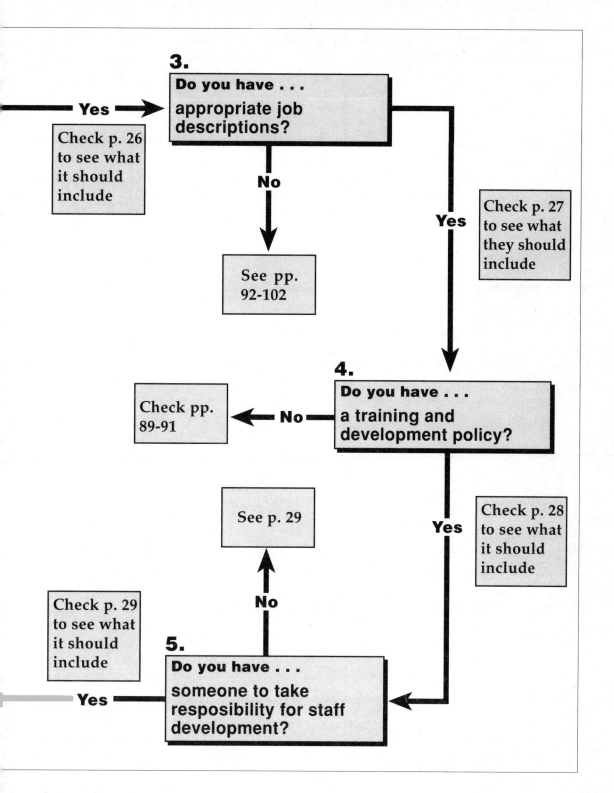

Yes ➡

Check p. 26 to see what it should include

3.

Do you have . . . appropriate job descriptions?

No

See pp. 92-102

Check p. 27 to see what they should include

Yes

4.

Do you have . . . a training and development policy?

No Check pp. 89-91

See p. 29

Check p. 28 to see what it should include

Yes

No

Check p. 29 to see what it should include

5.

Do you have . . . someone to take resposibility for staff development?

Yes

1. An Effective, Two-Way Communication System Involves

- staff having the opportunity to tell their manager when they feel that they need some input/assistance in a certain area;
- having the means through which this information will be listened to and acted upon;
- individuals receiving a reply to any query or request that is made, even if the request cannot be fulfilled;
- a means of enabling information from the base of the organisation to be communicated to the top, as well as enabling information to come 'down' from 'above'.

Activity

Do you have an effective two-way system of communication in your museum?

If so, list the evidence you can produce for it.

Do you still think you have an effective two-way system of communication?

If so, slot the details of this into your training and development ring-binder and refer back to the checklist.

If not, take time to think through the above guidelines and decide on the steps which you will take to do so.

2.   A Forward Plan Should

- be a 2–5-year programme for the museum, taking account of known and planned changes and developments;
- cover all aspects of museum work;
- prioritise specific objectives for each year of the plan providing long, medium and short-term aims;
- be the focus of a process which has assessed past and current operations, **engaged** all staff to ensure **ownership** of the plan, and **agreed** a set of costed and programmed objectives for the future which will fulfill the organisational needs long-term;
- be sufficiently **flexible** to allow for appropriate change or new opportunities to be accommodated;
- be comprehensive, in that all aspects of the functional areas should be integrated within it – e.g. collections care, conservation, financial management and training and development;
- rolled forward on an annual basis;
- include performance indicators against which progress can be monitored.

Note: If your museum is part of a Local Authority museum service the plan may either be part of the whole Authority plan or one that you develop yourself based on the information contained within the larger document.

Activity

Do you have a forward plan which does this?

If so, slot it into your training and development ring-binder and refer back to the checklist.

If you do not have any forward plan then take time to think through the above guidelines. If you work in a small museum see p. 35.

For further guidance on forward planning, please refer to *MGC Guidelines for Good Practice: Forward Planning*. Davies, 1996.

3. Effective Job Descriptions

- are based on a careful analysis of the job;
- have been reviewed recently;
- are tailored to the specifics of your museum service;
- provide a clear indication of what is expected of a member of staff;
- specify to whom the staff member reports;
- summarise the main knowledge, skills, attitudes and experiences required to perform the job to a competent level.

Activity

Do you have job descriptions which do this?

If so, slot these into your training and development ring-binder and refer back to the checklist.

If not, you can use the examples provided in the Tool Kit (see pp. 92-102) to consider and decide on the steps which you will take to do so. For example, you could consider reviewing your existing job descriptions against the appropriate S/NVQ standards.

4. A Training and Development Policy Should

- be a statement of training priorities at strategic level, i.e. a definition of how training relates and cross-refers to the objectives of the museum as a whole;
- include a statement of commitment to training and development for all staff and to communicating this throughout the museum;
- have a method for identifying staff needs on a regular basis, together with a known avenue through which staff can discuss their training needs both regularly and when they become apparent or are perceived by the staff member concerned;
- include an idea of how available financial resources can be allocated, e.g. through identified priorities or by an allocation to a specific service;
- include a commitment to undertake some form of quality control for training activities to ensure that only worthwhile means are used;
- state the means through which anyone who undertakes training or development can provide feedback.

A coherent policy will stress the positive personal development aspects of employment and provide a framework for personal job and organisational development covering:

- job analysis and description;
- recruitment and selection;
- induction and probation;
- supervision;
- appraisal;
- training.

Activity

Do you have a training and development policy which does this?

If so, slot it into your training and development ring-binder and refer back to the checklist.

If not, you can use the example provided in the tool kit (see pp. 89-91) to consider and decide on the steps which you will take to do so.

For further guidance on training policies, please refer to *MGC Guidelines for Good Practice: Managing Training in Museums*. Murch, 1997.

5. Someone Who Takes Responsibility for Staff Development Should

- know what the objectives and priorities of the museum are;
- monitor training and development needs throughout the museum on a regular basis;
- have responsibility for managing and dispersing the training budget to ensure an equal level of opportunity for all staff;
- be aware of and know how to apply for other possible bursaries and grants;
- keep up to date with legal and technical requirements, professional qualifications, changes in provision of training for museum staff, e.g. S/NVQs and AMA;
- provide information on available courses, exchange opportunities, professional updates, lectures, mandatory health and safety requirements, etc.;
- put people in touch with internal and external training/course providers and exchange opportunities/secondments;
- receive and ensure dissemination of feedback from those who have attended courses/exchanges/visits/secondments, etc.;
- ensure that records are kept showing staff attendance/participation in development and training opportunities – who has been where, to do what, how often, etc.;
- maintain confidentiality.

Activity

Do you have someone with responsibility for training who does this?

If so, slot the details of their responsibilities (e.g. their job description) into your training and development ring-binder and refer back to the checklist.

If not, take time to think through the above guidelines and decide on the steps which you will take to include these responsibilities in someone's role.

6.   A Training Budget Should

- have an adequate and recognised sum of money that is identified within the overall budget for the purpose of allowing staff to undertake training and development opportunities;
- be allocated and accounted for on a yearly basis;
- allow the in-house budget to be supplemented by external grants/bursaries/awards etc. for specific opportunities as and when they arise;
- recognise that if the museum is part of a Local Authority, then courses run by the Authority will be available at competitive rates and should be seen as an extension of the in-house resources dedicated to training and staff development.

Activity

Do you have a training budget which does this?

If so, slot details of your training budget into your training and development ring-binder and refer back to the checklist.

If not, take time to think through the above guidelines and decide on the steps which you will take to establish a training budget.

7. Regular Staff Review Should

- include a meeting between individual staff members and their line manager, usually on an annual basis, to review current work in line with the job description and forward plan for the museum;
- identify discrepancies between a job description and actual work undertaken (to ensure a response to changing demands in the service on an on-going basis). This might indicate a knowledge, skills or attitudinal gap that can be met by training or development;
- include agreement on a programme of work and development for the coming year with key objectives set, usually prioritised in some transparent way;
- provide an opportunity for the individual to talk through their concerns and observations and to offer suggestions in relation to their work and the museum as a whole;
- be followed up with a written agreement at the end of the appraisal detailing actions to be carried out by both parties during the next 12 months.

Note: 'Staff' is taken to mean all who work with the museum – paid or voluntary and in any capacity – e.g. Trustee/Guide.

Activity

Do you have regular staff review which does this?

If so, slot the details of this into your training and development ring-binder and refer back to the checklist.

If not, take time to think through the above guidelines and decide on the steps which you will take to consider regular staff review.

What gaps have you identified (if any) in your current approach to the management of training and development in your museum?

Who has responsibility for training and development in your museum currently?

Does this person have a detailed job description dealing with his or her training and development function?

          Yes   **No**

Are other staff and volunteers informed about this person's training and development function?

          Yes   **No**   **Partly?**

Do you have a training policy?

          Yes   **No**

What are the priorities of this policy (if you have one) or your current training and development activities in terms of:

a) skills

b) personal professional development for staff

c) types of activities supported?

What is your current budget for training and development?

How effectively do you think you use this?

What other resources are available to you to support training and development?

On the basis of the above, what do you see as the specific strengths and weaknesses of your current approach to training and development?

a) Strengths

b) Weaknesses

Taking these points into consideration, how would a TNA benefit:

a) your staff?

b) you?

c) your visitors and the museum as a whole?

Training and the Small Museum

Museums which do not yet have a forward plan, but which would like to learn new skills and participate in training and development, face a major challenge in training and development including the application of a TNA.

Small museums in particular may face difficulties which could make a systematic approach to identification of training needs a daunting task.

Shortage of people compared with the work to be done; perhaps absence of professionally qualified staff; slim budgets, reliance on volunteers; the demands presented by funding bodies can all be seen as pressures which the correct training and development programme based on effective analysis of training needs can help address. For such museums basic advice would be, **do not be put off by this book** – make a start by writing down all of the things which you do at present and assess or rate how well you are doing these.

Case Study

The Committee of a small volunteer-run museum had decided that they would like to change and update the displays (which had been in place for ten years), but the work involved seemed so daunting and expensive that they were at a loss as to where to begin. All of the Committee and volunteers (some 20 people) were called to a meeting to discuss what should be done. It soon became clear, however, that this challenge could not be considered in isolation. For example, the temporary store room was so full of items that no-one was quite sure what was in there or what the condition of the items was. It was therefore decided that all aspects of the museum's work would have to be reviewed before the displays could be tackled.

Led by the Honorary Curator, everyone contributed to a list of all of the museum's current activities and it soon became clear that, whilst everyone felt that the tea room and shop were very good, the documentation, storage and display work were a cause for concern. As a result, these areas were identified as priorities. One member of the staff had received training in basic museum documentation but others could give only limited help to tackle the backlog of items or assess their condition without such training themselves.

It was agreed that in order to make the best use of very limited resources, one volunteer would attend a basic documentation course, one a preventive conservation course, one a security course and another a course in basic design and display. On their return to the museum, these individuals would use the skills and knowledge acquired to coach other volunteers. In addition, two volunteers visited the curator of the neighbouring Local Authority museum to find out how the stores were organised there.

Gradually, after a great deal of hard work, the store room was transformed and the morale and motivation of all the existing volunteers was increased significantly. In addition, the museum trust launched a fund-raising campaign in the community to enable some of the items which had deteriorated to be conserved professionally, and to raise funds to buy new display cases in the following financial year.

For example, you could divide your activities into categories such as 'always', 'most of the time', 'sometimes', 'never', or 'very well', 'good', 'poor', 'very poor', etc. This process will allow you to identify your strengths and weaknesses, and areas in which you may wish to improve or change things. In other words you have arrived at a list of possible training and development needs.

It is important, however, that you do this by calling everyone together and giving them the opportunity to contribute, and p. 58 of Chapter 7 will give you some guidance on how to conduct such a group discussion.

Now that you have reviewed your performance you can transfer these into the form of an Action Plan for your museum. (If you are based in Scotland you might be considering or already have carried out the same method as part of the Guide to Service Quality for Visitor Attractions). You can use the example on p. 38 as a guide.

Training and development opens up the possibilities of change – if you do not have a forward plan or job descriptions etc. you can still develop your staff/volunteer skills and knowledge and take part in training activities. As you tackle one area of concern (e.g. your documentation backlog) you can follow this up with another. This will raise questions such as which should be tackled first, what impact will this have on how other work in the museum is carried out, and how can this be paid for? In time, you might find it beneficial to be able to make these decisions within an overall framework of what the museum wants to achieve – in other words through a forward plan. It is important, however, that you make a start and harness all of the commitment and enthusiasm within your group.

The benefits of being clear about your staff and volunteer training needs – and your own – should be self-evident.

Activity

On the next page you will find a Health Check form which has been partially completed. Complete the headings section for your museum and use this to review the activities with all the volunteers.

Small Museums – Health Check Form

Area of Activity	Very Good	Good	Poor	Very Poor
Health and Safety procedures				
Visitor care				
Security procedures				
Documentation				

Training and the Volunteer

Many museums are completely run by volunteers, or rely on voluntary help. In larger museums, volunteers sometimes occupy key positions in visitor care (within the reception areas, guiding, etc.) or they may work behind-the-scenes, assisting with various jobs which the visitor does not see. In a volunteer-run museum all the tasks are carried out by volunteers.

This book is very relevant for the volunteer. Team work is referred to throughout and the volunteer, once accepted, is part of the museum team. If he or she appears before the public then visitors will expect very much the same level of service as from any other member of staff.

Increasingly, other organisations which also rely on volunteer help are working towards the concept of the 'professional volunteer', and volunteer vocational qualifications are being introduced. This may at first appear to be a contradiction in terms, but in effect what it says is that if any organisation accepts volunteers then it has a duty to provide those volunteers with training, and they in turn have a duty to act in a professional manner. In this respect, museums should be no different.

> **Note: the areas detailed here are of equal relevance – whether or not the museum is itself a volunteer-run organisation, whether the museum has only one or two volunteers or whether it is a large museum with dozens of volunteers.**

Selection and recruitment

Does the museum have a policy on this or does it recruit on a first-come first-served basis? The museum may have had an excellent volunteer who has moved on. Ideally, the museum would like someone to replace him but it can hardly advertise for 'someone like Dan'. If a job description existed then this process would be much easier. If the museum does not have this then such factors as charm, confidence, or good presentation skills may influence judgment – something which might prove to be a mistake when the volunteer actually starts working in the museum.

A job description will not only help, but it may indicate to the volunteer what the museum really wants. This could result in fewer offers of help, put it could also result in recruiting a volunteer who comes into the post with 'both eyes open'. No one wants to turn away volunteers but it is much better that they join the museum knowing the reality of what it can offer rather than living in a dream that will turn sour and cause both parties needless disturbance.

Induction

Volunteers in particular need effective induction into the system. They may have only a very hazy notion of what the museum actually does. This may be based on coming as visitors, bringing children and friends with them.

Role clarification

This is important for all staff but critical for volunteers. They will bring a great deal of enthusiasm and goodwill which can soon evaporate unless their particular role in the museum is clarified. It is important to spell out what they are **not** expected to do. This may sometimes be a disappointment to them since they may enter with the aim of doing almost everything and great tact will be required. Role clarification should also include such aspects as volunteer times, duty rosters etc.

Health and Safety induction and training

It is a legal requirement that everyone should be aware of their responsibilities both to themselves, their colleagues and to visitors under the Health and Safety at Work Act (1974) and associated Guidelines and Codes. Volunteers are not exempt from these obligations.

Security and emergency training

In small museums where scarcity of funds is an issue, then the volunteers who look after the collection may be the main security precaution in place. In larger museums, a well-intentioned but untrained volunteer could prove to be a weak link in the security and emergency chain.

Dress code

Advise on appearance at work. Volunteers must look the part and feel the part.

Specialist knowledge

Some volunteers bring specialist knowledge with them – especially knowledge of the local area, certain types of machinery, equipment or industrial processes, or about living in a 'bygone age'. For any one of these categories, the volunteer tends to have the knowledge because they have lived or worked in an area for a long time or because they simply have a long life experience. In this situation it is important to plan for the future as the knowledge that these people have needs to be passed on before it is lost. Younger volunteers will need to learn from older ones.

   These aspects of training will require a proper approach. An individual should be responsible for volunteers to ensure that there is a progression through these items. In their first weeks in the job, arranging for a new volunteer to shadow an experienced member of staff can be very helpful.

Appraisal

It is recommended that appraisal interviews should be offered to all volunteers. Such interviews, as indicated earlier in this book, should show up any difficulties encountered in the role and ideas for developing it. In such a discussion, training needs may well arise. There is no reason why such an appraisal could not take the form of a focused group discussion. Indeed, it may be more comfortable for all if that were the case.

The volunteer's duty to the museum

Some museums have had a poor experience of volunteers because after an initial burst of enthusiasm and commitment, they have pulled out. A lack of proper role clarification, training and induction may well have been responsible. However, it is important to remember that a volunteer who comes forward and is accepted understands that this represents a commitment.

The more a volunteer can be made to feel a valued member of a team, the more such commitment will grow. It is usually those volunteers who have not been made welcome or who have been given the impression that the hours they contribute do not count for much who are most prone to stay away, go home early, take short cuts and generally leave other staff dissatisfied.

Some museums award Volunteer Cards (such as the one offered by the National Trust for Scotland) to all those who volunteer satisfactorily for a number of hours/days. Such cards enable the volunteer to bring along a friend free into the property of the Trust. Such a scheme is a move towards the 'professional volunteer'– commitment on both sides and a recognition in a non-cash way of their value to the organisation. Museums may not be able to offer something similar but some form of recognition will assist in the move towards creating a group of volunteers who feel accepted, involved and recognised for the valuable work they do.

5. Preparing to Conduct a TNA

Now that you have decided to conduct a Training Needs Analysis (TNA), you will have to consider the practicalities of setting one up, and identify the questions and decisions that will have to be asked and taken before you begin the process. Everyone has doubts about organising what, in the first instance, will be an 'extra' piece of work. But looking at staff development in a coherent way does not have to be an extra burden on the museum and its limited resources. Indeed, if training is not considered coherently then it is possible that resources will be wasted.

When considering a TNA it is vital to consult all those staff who may be affected, and to do this at the planning stage.

A TNA is a process in which all staff participate, not something which is done to them! As such it can result in increased motivation throughout staff as each individual reassesses his/her own attitude to the job.

A TNA which is 'sprung' on staff, catching them by surprise can create all kinds of negative impressions. They may think: 'What have we done to deserve this? Is this some reflection on the way in which we do our work? Is there a hidden agenda?'

It is most important then, that the staff should be involved in the TNA from the beginning. This might be achieved by starting with a meeting of the entire staff in which it is explained what the TNA is and what it is intended to do. Staff can ask any immediate questions, and they can contribute suggestions for carrying out the TNA which can be fed into the planning process.

It is important, however, to provide an additional opportunity for staff to come back with their worries, queries etc. after they have had time to reflect on the issues presented. This can often reveal genuine concerns which may not have been apparent at the larger meeting. Use can be made of anonymous feedback or comment sheets. It may be useful at this stage to encourage the museum/team to provide a time so that questions can be raised and suggestions made.

Before finalising the TNA, great care needs to be taken over the way in which it is to proceed. It is strongly recommended that consultation with staff is built in all along the way.

Face-to-face communication with staff is much more likely to produce results in terms of communication and sharing of concerns than memos and notices.

In larger museums, one practical step in this consultation process might be to set up a liaison group drawn from all sections of the museum to represent a wide range of interests. The purpose of this group would be to act as a sounding board as to how the TNA should be conducted.

The TNA process should be developed from the bottom up rather than from the top down.

This liaison group can assist in the drawing up of ground rules for the carrying out of the TNA, including such aspects as:

- issues of confidentiality – who should see what?
- who should receive copies of the report?
- when can staff comment on the draft report?
- what will be the staff's involvement in carrying out any recommendations?

The group can also advise on possible time-frames, practical aspects of carrying out interviews, and distributing and collecting any questionnaires.

Staff who feel threatened by the TNA, or who are kept in the dark about what it all entails, will not respond well to interviews and questionnaires.

If the consultation has been carried out productively, it is possible to receive a 100% return rate on all questionnaires and full attendance at any interviews or group/section meetings which may be convened to carry out the TNA.

Getting Down to Basics: Essential Questions to Ask

Effective preparation is all about thinking out clearly why something needs to be done and then in detail how best to achieve it.

Activity
Write down some of the basic questions which you think you should ask before setting up a TNA in your museum.

Compare your list with these questions and answers.

Question: Why a TNA? Don't you already know enough about what training needs there are? Is there not enough material about for you to avoid having to go through all this work and expense? Can you just have a sample of staff in and talk to them, or better still, spend a little more time observing what is going on in the museum and find out where the gaps are?

Answer: You will know quite a lot about the training needs of the staff but a TNA can provide an opportunity to take a fresh look. A TNA is like drawing a line, providing a benchmark against which skills development can be measured.

Question: Who is going to do the work?

Answer: There are a number of options here. First of all, you can do it yourself with the assistance of your own colleagues or, if appropriate, you can ask staff from a similar neighbouring museum to carry it out. You could seek advice from an Area Museum Council, your curatorial advisor or if your funds permit you can pay external consultants to do it.

Question: How are you going to get it done? What about the logistics?

Answer: This is where the preparation comes in. Read on . . .

Question: How are you going to make use of the information that will be collected by the TNA?

Answer: It is important to start thinking of this well before the TNA is completed. There is little point in going to all the effort of conducting a TNA for the results to be buried or put on a shelf. Similarly, there may be a need to produce a summary of the main points and to give this out to all staff.

A number of other questions may have arisen, but this process of thinking up questions about the TNA should make your position clearer when the time comes to brief others – external consultants, staff from other museums, local authorities, or other members of staff.

Who is going to do the work?

Are there other specific advantages and disadvantages in respect of these options in your particular situation – if so, list them.

	Advantages	Disadvantages
Staff of own museum		
Colleagues from another museum		
External consultants		

The decision about who to use to carry out the TNA is a difficult one. It may be that some combination of an outside consultant or advisor working with a staff member is possible, or that this team could be enriched by having someone from another museum as a counter weight.

One final point to note, the manager has not been included in this process, which might at first appear odd, given his/her overall responsibility for staff. As a TNA is a fresh look at training, however, it must include the views of the manager. Hence, it is important that he/she is not involved in carrying out all the information gathering. This will ensure that the manager is also asked about his or her training needs – something which is quite commonly omitted or overlooked.

45

Activity

What resources are available to you?

Write these down below.

In spite of all the careful planning, things may go wrong. It is very important that a rapid, reliable and effective communication system is set up between those carrying out the TNA and the staff.

Much confusion can arise if there are delays in, or disruption to, the interviewing schedule etc. It is well worth considering measures such as bulletin boards or a special 'TNA memo'.

Activity

List the means of communication you intend to adopt to publicise and keep staff informed about the TNA and identify the specific resource requirements of these.

6. Checklist of Practicalities

Initiating a TNA in a museum environment is no different from planning a new exhibition or any other self-contained project which requires planning and managing in order to effect a successful outcome. It is useful to think of a TNA in these terms and to use the five principles of project management as the framework around which to build the Analysis.

For those unfamiliar with project management there are five stages:

1. **Feasibility**: the stage prior to action where an idea becomes a fully resourced reality.
2. **Initiation**: the who, what, why, when and how of the project are sorted out at this stage.
3. **Live running**: the time when the work that has been planned is carried out within a specified budget and time-scale.
4. **Closure**: a short period when the project is formally wound up and results handed over.
5. **Review**: happens at a later stage when the formal benefits of having undertaken the project can be evaluated.

Feasibility

Putting project management into practice means that there are some important questions that the manager needs to ask before actually implementing the TNA programme. Remember, the TNA does not happen in isolation. Go back to the checklist on pp. 22-23 to reconsider whether the necessary support systems are in place to make carrying out a TNA worthwhile.

Activity

The following checklist summarises all the preliminary thoughts to consider before starting.

- Do I have the necessary mechanisms in place to support the findings of a TNA?
- Why do I want to carry out a TNA, where does it fit into the museum's plans?

- When would it be most beneficial to carry out the TNA?
- What do I hope to get from this in relation to staff training and development?
- What are the specifics and what overall impressions do I need to find out?
- Who is going to be involved – the whole museum or one section?
- What resource implications are there and can these be met through internal and/or external sources?
- How will I ensure that follow-up happens?

Write down your answers in the box below.

Planning checklist

Initiation

Once the answers to these questions are clear, the next step is to put a small team together who will be responsible for undertaking the TNA, with one person taking overall charge. In small museums, the team may only consist of one or two people. This team will need to work out a plan of action and should consider the following questions when drawing up their framework.

Activity
- Are we clear about the aims of the TNA?
- What other information already exists that we can use?
- What do we need to find out from staff and how are we going to do this?
- Do we have the skills available to carry out the TNA in-house and if not where can we get these from?
- How long will it take?

Write down your answers in the box provided below.

Initiation checklist

In constructing the plan for the TNA, there are three distinct stages:

1. getting the sample sorted out and choosing what methods to use;
2. collecting the information required;
3. collating and analysing data to make sense of it.

Sample

Everyone needs to have the opportunity to contribute to the TNA. It is probable, therefore, that unless everyone can be interviewed, some form of written information – e.g. a questionnaire or a log – will have to be used. If it is decided to use interviewing as part of the package, then the feasibility of doing this must be considered carefully. For example, how many people can realistically be interviewed in the time available and what can be gained from face-to-face contact that cannot be obtained from a written form?

Choosing which methods to use

All of the different techniques that can be used to collect information from staff, volunteer and documentary sources are summarised in Chapter 7. Each technique has its advantages and disadvantages and some will be more appropriate to the available expertise than others. Similarly, methods which may be suitable for a museum based in one building may be less appropriate if staff are based in a number of locations. The numbers and types of staff to be included in the TNA will also be a deciding factor. A city museum and gallery service with 20 or more staff will be more likely to use a wider range of tools than a smaller, more intimate setting where there are only one or two permanent staff and volunteers.

Collecting the information required

Whatever methods are chosen, the actual collection of the information needs to be carried out with as little disruption to the running of the museum as possible. There is no point in looking at what training needs staff have if, whilst carrying out the survey, all of your visitors have been driven away because there was no-one there to look after them, or stress levels in staff and volunteers have been raised because of the extra burden the TNA has placed on them.

This means that shadowing and interviewing should be carried out at a mutually convenient time and place; questionnaires and logs are requested for return after a reasonable but not too lengthy amount of time – usually 10 days or a fortnight; and documentation should be collected and studied throughout the course of the TNA. In other words, care is taken to make the process as painless as possible for participants.

Remember: all the work that goes into collecting information has to be carried out within the time-scale that has been set and within the budget that has been allocated.

Plan well, because if all of the interviews cannot be completed, or help is needed with putting a questionnaire together and neither has been budgeted for, then the remit will not be fulfilled and the quality of the TNA data will suffer.

Collating and analysing the data

Do not collect more data than you can handle!

It is all too easy on finishing the actual survey, to be faced with mounds of paper that engender panic instead of satisfaction that staff have participated so thoroughly. If time to analyse the TNA findings is likely to be limited, this should be taken into account when planning what methods to use.

The aim is a concise, understandable and, above all, useful document which can inform the museum's future training plans. A long, rambling list of what people said or who does what is of little use. Remember, the TNA is about trying to match where the museum is now, with where it wants to be in the future, and to look at possible solutions to bridge the gaps.

The TNA report should be concise and readable. It should be summarised into no more than 2 to 4 sides of A4 paper and all staff should receive a copy of this. The full report can be circulated to those that need it (i.e. managers) and made available to anyone else who requests to see it.

Closure

How can you mark the end of the project?

The work is finished, the written summary has been handed over and a short presentation of the findings and recommendations should be given to those who took part.

It is always useful to put the final report into a draft form at first. Information from these short meetings can actually inform the document and make it necessary to make minor amendments. People will feel a greater ownership of the findings if they feel that they have been part of the whole process and not just 'used' as sources of information. So often, after reports have been written and presentations made, nothing appears to happen. This can lead to a mood of cynicism amongst staff who have given up their time for interviews and for filling in questionnaires – in addition to having had their awareness/expectations raised about what they might be able to do, or future training needs.

A good way of announcing the closure of the project, therefore, is to follow up some of the recommendations almost straight away, so that people can see that it was not just a 'paper exercise'. Remember, the reason the TNA happened in the first place was because you, as a manager, decided that it should be undertaken. This implies commitment, and therefore action.

It may be something relatively simple like making sure courses are publicised to everyone and not just circulated to a few people, or a new form could be drawn up so that a record of everyone's training needs and achievements can be recorded accurately. Larger, more fundamental actions that have been highlighted will take more time, as they will need to feed into the museum's forward plan. But remember:

Always let people know what you are doing.

Review

In relation to a TNA, the process of review is almost implicit. The whole point of the exercise is to introduce a more structured, needs-orientated and monitored training programme to the museum. Future activity should therefore be reviewed at individual level routinely. As discussed in other chapters of this book, analysis of training and development needs should not just be seen as a one-off, independent process. It should be integrated into a museum-wide process of commitment to career development and review and regular appraisal/performance management.

If you opt to undertake a complete museum review, this should not have to be repeated more than every five years or so, if recommendations from the TNA are acted upon and monitored. Times and requirements change, however, and it cannot be assumed that one TNA will serve the purpose for ever! If particular chapters or topics were highlighted in this TNA as areas of concern, then reassessing the situation in these specific locations after 6 months or a year would be advisable.

Remember the five stages:

1. Feasibility
2. Initiation
3. Live running
4. Closure
5. Review

Activity

Taking into account all the relevant influences, what steps can you take to introduce the systematic approach to TNA in your museum or to make your current approach more coherent and effective?

List these and identify a possible time-scale for such activity.

Step	Date

7. Techniques: The Options Available

Before starting a TNA you will have to consider the different techniques and methods that are available to collect information.

Your choice of methods will be determined partly by personal preference, but also by practical constraints such as the expertise available, time and motivation.

In deciding what methods to use, certain considerations have to be made:

1. Any information that you collect should be useful in meeting the aims of the TNA, i.e. it should help to determine where the museum and its staff are now, and where they should be/wish to be in the future.

2. Read through all the options before you choose what methods to use. By doing this you can see what is practical and feasible for your particular setting. There is no prescription for collecting the information that you require; you just need to be sensible.

3. When considering each method, think:
   - can we do that or do we know someone who could help with it?
   - does this fit in with our pattern of work?
   - would it be easier to bring someone in to do this?
   - will the staff respond to/feel comfortable with this?
   - do we have the resources to do this?

4. Decide who you have in-house that can design and implement the different methods to be used. If you lack expertise in a certain area or cannot spare the staff time then consider using people from another museum, external consultants or advisors (see p. 45 for details).

5. More than one method should be used. Do not rely solely on using a questionnaire or interviewing everyone. If you collect information using more than one source, you can cross-check things as they arise and it makes it more likely that you will pick up a broader selection of data to inform the survey. In addition, because you are trying to look at where you are now and identify the gaps between this situation and future needs, information is required from staff about their perceptions of need, as well as factual evidence of known and supposed changes.
   If you decide to interview people, you are collecting information from them that they remember at that particular time and place. In addition, they cannot tell someone of things they may not be aware of, whether in

writing or verbally. Other ways of gathering training needs and gaps are therefore needed in order to supplement this type of data.

6. Choose methods that will allow all staff (paid, unpaid, volunteers and management committees) the opportunity to take part in the TNA – but remember that each person has a right to refuse if they so wish.

7. What methods you choose to use will depend partly on how many staff and volunteers you have working in the museum. The most productive and therefore preferred method, is some form of dialogue – whether discussion, direct observation or interview, but it is not always possible to see everyone personally.
    With smaller numbers (less than 10) it will be easy enough to talk to everybody either in a formal or informal way. Where there are much larger numbers of staff within staff groups – most probably attendants and curators, then it is not necessary to speak to everyone individually and a combination of interviews, small group discussions, questionnaires and observation will prove useful.

8. A TNA is unusual in terms of surveys, in that it is preferable that everyone gets a chance to take part, i.e. you do not take a sample to exclude people, but to decide what type of response you will ask them to give. It is also unusual in that there is likely to be a high response rate for all methods used. In many other surveys, it is anticipated that a lot of people will not respond, but because of the nature of the information being collected, this tends not to be the case for training and development.

The following methods will be discussed:

*   Discussion groups;
*   Interviews: individual, pairs and groups;
*   Questionnaires: structured and semi-structured;
*   Logs: individual and team;
*   Observation: direct and indirect;
*   Self-assessment checklist;
*   Documentation;
*   Visitor surveys.

For each method, questions will be raised about why they should be used and in what situation, as well as describing their relative strengths and weaknesses.

Discussion Groups

Why a discussion group?

In some museums, there will not be enough staff available to make it worthwhile holding more formal interviews. If you only have 4 or 5 staff who all share the running of the museum to a greater or lesser extent, then a 'round table' discussion will be the most productive.

Groups of volunteers benefit from open discussion about their situation.

What does it involve?

1. All staff are gathered together and a chaired discussion is held during which some key questions about training are addressed. These questions will revolve around the type of issues covered in the interview schedule.
2. This differs from a group interview as there are people from different grades and jobs present. Whilst key issues are covered, everyone is encouraged/prompted to take part. The information given is more free-flowing around the central themes provided.

STRENGTHS
- Everyone in a small museum setting can get round the same table and discuss individual and shared training needs.
- It is not as limiting as formal interviews, it allows staff to set some of their own agenda in relation to prompts used.
- It allows all staff to make valued contributions to the discussion.
- It is particularly useful for volunteers.

LIMITATIONS
- The potential exists for different grades of staff to over-ride those whom they supervise/manage.
- The central issue might get left behind in the discussion without a good chairperson.
- It presents a difficulty for accurate recording by the chairperson as more than one person or idea may be involved at the same time.
- The detail of a specific job may get lost in the 'group' response.
- Senior staff may be inhibited in discussing long-term plans which may be sensitive to a certain job holder's position.

Summary

A group discussion is a valuable asset in developing team and group potential but needs careful chairing – preferably carried out by an outsider. The optimum number for this type of discussion is 8 people which may be the whole staff in a small museum or one section within one of the larger sites. Larger numbers can be seen together, however, if the chairperson is skilled enough.

Interviews – Individual/Paired/Group/Mobile
Why interview?

There are two main reasons for interviewing staff:

1. You can get more detailed information from people when you see them face-to-face. Any ambiguities can be sorted out and the volume of information will be greater than through a written questionnaire.
2. Some people find it difficult to complete written forms and offering them a questionnaire would be inappropriate. Not everyone likes to be observed at work, nor is it possible to observe everyone and interpret what they are doing.

What does interviewing involve?

1. People must be trained to be interviewers as it takes skill to gather and record information accurately. The person or people who construct the interview schedule should also have the relevant skills, as it is not as easy as it looks to ask the 'right' questions. The people chosen to interview must also command the trust and respect of staff if accurate answers are to be gained. The Tool Kit gives some information on the type of skills needed to undertake survey interviewing.
2. When interviewing staff, it is important to consider whether the people involved would benefit from being seen alone or with others. As a rule of thumb, the more senior people in the organisation would benefit from being seen alone as they will have both individual and organisational information to give, e.g. museum director, senior curators etc.
3. Those who do not hold a specific managerial responsibility can be seen in pairs or groups. The number that can be seen at any one time is dictated by two factors – how many people of the same grade/job type can be free at the same time, in the same place and how many the interviewer feels comfortable dealing with at once.
4. Staff interviewed together must be of the same job type, e.g. all attendants or sales staff etc. as this will assist the identification of common or team/department training needs. Decisions must be taken about whether their immediate supervisor or manager should be included in the group. Some people will feel comfortable if their manager is present but others will not.
5. Planning to see staff has to revolve around their duties, e.g. museum attendants can be seen together in the hours before opening time as a group, or individually throughout the day when duties allow. Depending on the job type, interviews can be in an allocated room (or corner of the museum) or on the move. The latter might be the case for smaller museums where attendant staff need to be seen whilst working or for people in peripatetic jobs where movement cannot be avoided.

6. Everyone has to be asked/given a chance to answer the same questions. Additional sheets should be used for the senior curators/directors of the museum in order to get a more strategic view of the organisation than from other staff who could not necessarily be expected to know about or feel in a position to comment.

What sort of questions should be asked?

The Tool Kit gives an example of an interview schedule that can be used for analysing training needs. This has been designed for use in the museum setting and allows a wide range of options to be explored with the interviewee(s). It can be used with all staff from curators, to museum attendants to volunteers etc. In addition, there is an extra sheet that should be used with heads of sections or directors which asks for the strategic view of the museum's future.

Individual interviews

STRENGTHS

- No-one else is there to listen in.
- Although structured to ensure reliability, an individual interview allows individual issues to be explored relevant to the overall theme of training.
- It is crucial in relation to the director's views on where the museum is going.
- It is a valuable way of gaining staff perceptions of training gaps (could sample according to job type).
- It invests time in the individual, which introduces a 'feel good' factor.
- It provides the opportunity to check out items that are poorly described in the first instance.

LIMITATIONS

- Time and cost.
- If you wish to be truly independent and anonymous then it requires someone external to the museum in question.
- Many of these criticisms could be eliminated if some form of on-going career review/staff appraisal was the norm.
- It only gathers the information that people remember at that particular time.
- Also some performance deficits that the individual may not be aware of are missed (mainly attitudinal).
- Some people find the format threatening.
- An interview is an artificial situation.

Small group interviews/pairs

STRENGTHS

- For people less used to being interviewed, a small group is less threatening.
- Groups allow people to spark off ideas from one another.
- They provide a chance to check things out between everyone at the same time.
- A wider sample is possible in the same amount of time, therefore they can be more cost-effective.
- They keep people of the same grade/job type together without supervisors/managers in situ.

LIMITATIONS

- They take a lot of people off the job at one time.
- The interviewer usually only takes one consensus view away so some individual detail may be lost.
- They are more complex to manage and they demand greater skill from the interviewer.
- The group may talk each other into the same opinions even though this may not originally have been the case.

Mobile interviews

STRENGTHS

- You do not have to take people away from their job.
- The interviewer gets the opportunity to see what people are doing, so that other issues relating to training may be highlighted that would be lost if interviewed in an office.

LIMITATIONS

- The interviewer has to be very skilled and also have a working knowledge of the job of the interviewee.
- A biased perception of the job may arise as you only see interviewees for a part of one day.

Summary

Interviews form a valuable part of any TNA but should be supplemented by other forms of information. The crucial aspect here is who carries out the interviews. It may be desirable to use interviewers outwith the immediate managerial line and it is suggested that either peers, possibly staff from another 'paired' museum or other, external people who have no position within the museum should be used.

Three different types of interview have been mentioned, some of which are more appropriate in different situations and for gathering different types of information than others. For instance, small group interviews may be valuable with junior/manual staff in providing a less intimidating atmosphere than the one-to-one interview. Various perspectives on the same training issue can be elicited, however, and care needs to be taken to avoid 'group think'. 'Mobile' interviews are useful in the context of museums where a lot of work is carried out on a peripatetic basis (in-house and/or between sites).

Questionnaires

Why a questionnaire?

1. It is not always possible or desirable to speak to everybody individually or in groups. In this instance, giving people a questionnaire is the best way to gather basic information from all employees.
2. Some museums will have large numbers of staff. In this instance, it is not necessary to speak to everyone and those that are not seen, should be given a questionnaire – again this makes sure that everyone is given an option to take part in the TNA.
3. If external or peer interviewers are used, not all staff will be present on the days appointed to carry out the interviews/observation etc., so questionnaires become the viable alternative.

What does it involve?

1. Questionnaires are not easy to design, so ensure that someone with experience should be consulted. The Tool Kit gives an example of a questionnaire that can be used.
2. Individuals should each be given their own questionnaire and left with instructions about where, when and to whom it should be returned. Confidentiality of responses must be guaranteed.
3. A time-scale should be set for the return of the form as it is all too easy to forget about it and 'leave it until tomorrow'. 10 days is a reasonable amount of time to give people to complete the questionnaire.

STRENGTHS
- **Questionnaires are able to reach a large number of staff within the museum.**
- **They are relatively cost-effective.**
- **They make sure that everyone gets asked exactly the same questions in a systematic way.**
- **They provide a good way of collecting quantitative as well as qualitative data.**
- **They can be completely anonymous and/or confidential if this is an issue.**

> **LIMITATIONS**
> - **There is no way to follow up illegible, incomplete or particularly interesting answers.**
> - **A questionnaire only gets answers to the questions asked, so they remain quite limited in scope.**
> - **They are an impersonal way of collecting information which some people find off-putting.**
> - **They can be relatively easy for people to ignore and not complete.**

Summary

Questionnaires are essential in any type of data collection, but should not be used on their own without corroboration from other sources. They are not, however, an easy option. Someone who has experience in questionnaire design must be involved at the preparatory stage of the document.

Training Logs – Individual and Team

Why a training log?

1. In order to capture information about situations for which people do not feel totally prepared, but were not necessarily aware of before the incident, a log can be used to record an individual's experiences.
2. Some people are responsible for a group of staff, and in addition to their own development needs, they will have an overview of their team's needs. In this instance a team log can help to capture this information.
3. A log is an active document and does not rely on what people can remember that they have experienced. It identifies current situations and adds to the depth of information that can be collected to highlight development needs.

What does it involve?

1. The essence of a log is that people take notes of any situation that they come across at work over a specified period of time (for example a week or 10 days), when they feel that they are unable to cope to their satisfaction. These instances could be practical, inter-personal, technical etc. In noting the situation they are then asked to suggest what they feel would help to remedy the deficit, so that in future they would be more able to cope.
2. What is being noted here is the mismatch between current skill and the experience at hand. This in turn points to a potential learning situation and, therefore, a possible training/development need.

3. Two different types of log are included in the Tool Kit, one for individual use and one for use by a team manager, i.e. head keeper, head attendant etc. The former picks up specific, personal needs and the latter the possible needs of a team (however small or large). Personal requirements as well as those which are more strategic are thus identified.

Individual log

STRENGTHS

- A log catches everyday situations that people find themselves in, where they may not have realised that they had a training need.
- It prompts people to reflect on their practice as they are actually doing things, not in an artificial situation like an interview.
- It can be used as a personal record that the individual completes and then uses as a structure for the basis of a discussion at appraisal or in a TNA interview, thus allowing them to keep what could be seen as shortcomings in their practice to themselves.

LIMITATIONS

- A log is dependent on the individual being able to identify possible gaps in their practice.
- If someone has a particular problem area, e.g. attitudinal they may not perceive this themselves and would therefore not identify the deficiency.

Team log

STRENGTHS

- As above except that it cannot be used as a personal record.
- It prompts the supervisor/manager to look constructively at their team's practice.
- It allows particular problem areas with individuals to be identified by the manager which can then be discussed with the staff member, as well as providing a team needs profile.

LIMITATIONS

- It may be seen by some team staff as threatening and judgmental.
- It is dependent on the manager being able to identify possible gaps.

Summary

The log is useful for collecting otherwise unforeseeable information. It makes people stop and think about what they are doing and actively involves them in suggesting possible solutions to their perceived needs. It is particularly beneficial as people complete it when they are 'on the job' and actively involved in their daily duties.

Training Needs Observation
Why training needs observation?

1. Observation aims to collect more in-depth information in the same way that the log does. By 'shadowing' people as they actually carry out their work, the observer can ask questions as people are doing their duties, and engage in discussion as work is under way. A different set of responses will be obtained using this method than is obtained from an interview or through a questionnaire.
2. This method is an extension of the individual interview technique and ideally should be used once a baseline of information has been collected through interview, relevant to specific job types.

What does it involve?

1. An observer agrees to 'shadow' a member of staff around the museum for a morning or an afternoon. They record what actions they see the person involved in and ask questions about the experience and knowledge needed to carry out these duties and how what they are doing relates to their job description.
2. The staff member is asked to describe their job and then questioned in detail about what training they have already received, how they have learned to do the job and what further needs they feel are apparent.
3 The member of staff is later interviewed, if possible, to ask further questions from the interview schedule about training/development opportunities and how they see their job developing.

STRENGTHS
- **Training needs observation catches everyday situations that people find themselves in, where they may not have realised that they had a training need.**
- **It prompts people to reflect on their practice as they are actually doing things, not in the more formal interview situation.**
- **It allows an observer to draw out potential training needs.**
- **It allows a longer amount of time to be spent with a staff member thereby giving the opportunity for a more in-depth view to be taken.**

LIMITATIONS
- **It has cost and time implications.**
- **A biased perception of the job may arise as the observer only sees staff for a part of one day.**
- **It can only be carried out with a small sample.**
- **'Observer effect', i.e. the influence that the observer has on what is done or how it is done.**

Summary

It is possible with this method that the member of staff being observed might feel that they are part of a time and motion study. Care must therefore be taken to eliminate this possibility. The value of the method lies in the potential for drawing out information that would otherwise go unnoticed.

Self-Assessment Checklist

Why self-assessment?

1. It is often the case that the individual is the best person to assess their needs, since they can often pinpoint quite accurately where their strengths and weaknesses lie.
2. A self-assessment checklist can easily be developed using the basis of the units and elements of competence of Scottish/National Vocational Qualifications.
3. Information gained in this way can be used to supplement other data that is collected. Such an approach could also be integrated with a staff development programme focused on individual need.

What does it involve?

The individual is asked to rate themselves according to a pre-defined schedule against performance criteria, related to some elements of competence. For instance, the following scale is often used:

1 = I am competent and can produce evidence to prove this;
2 = I am competent but unsure regarding producing evidence of this;
3 = I am not yet competent in this area.

STRENGTHS
- **The resulting information provides a clear picture of the person's current perceived ability against the criteria that have been chosen for the checklist.**
- **A repeat self-assessment at regular intervals can provide information which allows the individual to accurately highlight where their competency is improving over time, as well as continuing to pinpoint what areas they need to work on.**

> **LIMITATIONS**
> - **If a person has a 'blind spot' about deficiencies in their performance they will not be able to rate themselves accordingly.**
> - **This can result in areas of need remaining unrecognised unless discussion with a third party highlights the potential problem.**

Summary

Self-assessment provides an additional tool for defining specific areas of need against recognised competencies for the individual.

Documentation

Why documentation?

1. In order to be able to understand the context of the training needs and to be able to prioritise any findings, it is important to use existing documents which chart the museum's functions and future developments.
2. Existing information about training plans or appraisal techniques in use should be used to inform the analysis and to place the results into context.
3. Other literature which relates to the museum world about what training and development opportunities are required or available will help in offering solutions to perceived training and development needs, e.g. vocational qualifications.
4. There may be other reports available that relate to the museum and its activities which will provide helpful background information to the TNA.

What does it involve?

1. The museum's forward plan should be consulted for the short, medium and long-term aims of the museum.
2. Job descriptions are needed to see whether the people in the post meet the requirements of the job.
3. Other literature should be studied to ensure sound solutions are offered to cover the gaps and needs that are identified by the survey.

- A TNA should have job descriptions in place (or some other way of describing the job, e.g. targets, objectives, key areas etc.), in order to be able to begin the process of assessing the needs of the individual or a group of individuals. Job descriptions, where they exist, should be up to date, accurate and reflect the demands of the actual job.
- Other documentation as outlined in the checklist on pp. 22-23 should also be available.

Summary

This is a necessary part of any methodological package in order to provide a context and inform the process of investigation.

Visitor Surveys

Why visitor surveys?

1. These are a specific example of documentation that can be particularly helpful for two reasons. One is the direct feedback that they contain on visitors' perceptions of the museum. They let you know whether people are happy with the level of service, type of displays, level of interpretation, cafe facilities, disabled access etc. Depending on the responses, individual staff groups can be identified as having training and development needs or the museum can seek to address particular deficits which may in turn have training implications.

2. The second reason why visitor surveys can be helpful is in the design of questionnaires and interviews to be used with staff. Information that has been collected about visitor numbers, age distribution of visitors, busiest days etc., can be included in questionnaires to find out whether staff have a realistic perception of their visitors.

What do these involve?

Surveys of this kind may be carried out routinely by in-house staff or on a more selective basis using outside agencies. They involve asking a sample of visitors a specific set of questions about the museum, its exhibits and facilities etc. in order to assess their satisfaction with the level of service.

STRENGTHS
- Surveys make important information available that reflects the visitors' views of the museum.
- The public voice is a powerful argument when looking at possible areas for improvement.
- They provide a different perspective on what the museum is doing and how it is meeting its aims, which staff can then discuss in terms of future developments.

LIMITATIONS
- They only provide information on specific issues that have been explored.
- They do not allow dialogue between visitors and museum staff.

Summary

Visitor surveys are important in providing extra information from a third party about the functioning of the museum. They can feed into some of the questioning and discussion that takes place in analysing training needs.

Activity

What expertise/sources of information do you have readily available within your museum for implementing any of these methods for your TNA?

Which techniques/methods will you select to collect your TNA data?

8. Action Planning

Analysis

Once you have collected the information that you require, you need to produce a concise and meaningful written report that will provide the museum with training and development options for its staff. It is wise to be aware, however, that some of the findings will point to changes that should be considered within the organisational structure of the museum, i.e. they are not strictly related to training and development. See this as a bonus! Nothing exists in isolation so training and development will need to be seen in the broad context which is bound to include communication, management structures etc.

This will mean looking at all the sheets of information and deciding what individual, section and organisational training and development needs have been highlighted by the survey. From looking through people's responses, patterns will emerge about needs that are apparent for a group of staff or for an individual. These will need to be prioritised against the information contained in the forward plan and the knowledge that you now have about the museum's future needs and individual staff members' aspirations.

The Tool Kit gives a suggested format for summarising the needs of staff which can be used as part of the training strategy and related quality control processes.

Action Planning

Having committed yourself to the TNA, collected the information and produced an analysis of the results with some level of prioritisation attached, you now need to work on integrating this into your overall museum strategy.

This will require some level of **Action Planning**, a useful approach which includes focusing on objectives or goals.

Techniques such as Management by Objectives or tools such as **SMART goals** are probably familiar to you already, but it may be worth thinking about the benefits of applying them to TNA itself.

Action Planning using these techniques is a necessary complement to any strategic or corporate planning that you engage in which addresses training and development.

Such Action Planning can be based on objectives which:

- permit unified planning;
- serve as a basis for motivation;
- enable management to perform the function of control;
- provide a sense of achievement.

Management by Objectives is particularly useful in respect of the training and development function insofar as it must involve discussion and agreement of specifications. It also forces planning; communications into action; includes people and focuses effort and is therefore quite compatible with a positive approach to training and development in the museum. SMART goals may be seen as equally relevant to action planning, insofar as they require that goals should be:

- **S**pecific, i.e. should state exactly what the person is responsible for;
- **M**easurable, i.e. state how performance is going to be measured and what a good outcome looks like;
- **A**ttainable, i.e. be reasonable and related to what has happened in the past;
- **R**elevant, i.e. address an activity that makes a difference in overall performance;
- **T**rackable, i.e. able to be measured frequently by an effective record keeping system.

Clearly your own action plan will relate to the specific circumstances your museum finds itself in at the moment, your aspirations for the future and the dynamic of staff and the environment in which they operate.

However, an action plan should nonetheless help you manage the training and development function and may be an aid to your own self-development as a manager.

It is essential that an action plan along the lines outlined addresses:

- resourcing;
- monitoring;
- evaluation.

and it may be that the use of performance indicators in such a plan will help you gauge progress.

Of course there are existing **points of reference** which can help you with the process of systematically identifying and responding to or even anticipating training needs and development. Examples of these are listed below.

Assessment against external standards

You could use the **Registration Scheme for Museums and Galleries in the United Kingdom** as the catalyst to developing your museum's objectives and policies (further information can be obtained from the Museum & Galleries Commission or from your Area Museum Council – addresses contained in Sources and Resources).

Or, if you are confident that you have the components of staff development in place, you might like to consider introducing the opportunity for staff to gain Scottish/National Vocational Qualifications.

(Further details of the museum sector VQs can be obtained from the Museum Training Institute, and on other sectors which may be appropriate (such as retailing) from the Scottish Qualifications Authority or the Qualifications and Curriculum Authority (see Sources and Resources).

You might also like to consider having your system assessed against the Investors in People award. Investors in People is the national standard for effective training and development which aims to help organisations improve their performance through having effective staff development systems in place. Further information can be obtained from Training and Enterprise Councils/Local Enterprise Companies. The Museum Training Institute has produced a practical book for museums, galleries and heritage organisations entitled *Achieving Investors in People*. (See Further Reading.)

Activity
What would be the benefits (and costs) to your museum of utilising external standards?

Quality focused development

You could begin to look at developing and/or refining the museum's recruitment procedures, or senior staff's interviewing skills.

You could look towards refining the criteria against which you use to select training providers to deliver any staff training internally. For example, now that you have completed the book you should be able to be more focused on exactly what you want the trainer to cover, and will be able to spot an attempt to sell you an 'off-the shelf' training package. You could address how best to develop the staff's coaching skills to enable much more training to be undertaken within the museum itself.

Activity

What are the key areas of quality improvement you would like to pursue in respect of training and development needs, their identification and satisfaction?

Begin to create your own Action Plan by working through the following set of activities.

Activity

List the six most significant or important training and development needs for your museum as a whole.

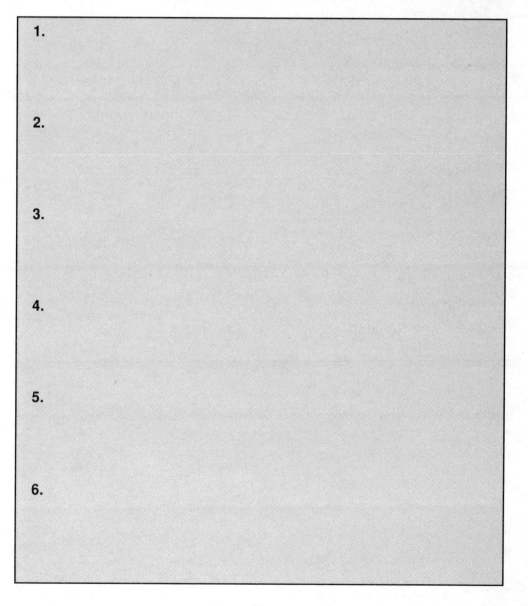

1.

2.

3.

4.

5.

6.

Activity

Select four staff or volunteers doing different jobs or performing different functions at different levels and list their specific training and development needs.

PERSON A

Job title or function

PERSON B

Job title or function

PERSON C

Job title or function

PERSON D

Job title or function

Activity

List similarities and differences in respect of the needs of individuals identified above.

Select two units or teams and identify their specific training and development needs

SECTION A

Function

SECTION B

Function

Activity

Now review the identified needs of:

- individuals;
- teams;
- the museum as a whole.

What similarities and differences came into focus? List these.

What are the management implications of this comparison?

Activity

Now return to your original list of the six most significant training and development needs of your museum as a whole (noted on p. 75). Are they still valid? If so, what evidence can you present to support your prioritisation of them? If not, make a new list and identify the source of evidence on which it is based.

Now that you have read this book and identified training needs for your museum, consider the following steps.

Review what training and development options are available.

Match these to the training and development needs.

Plan to secure and/or allocate the required resources.

Decide what you need to do to improve your approach to TNA and rank these in order of priority.

9. What Next?

At this stage of the book you should be in a position to make some positive moves with the information that you have collected and the action planning that you have undertaken.

If you have carried out a TNA of the entire museum, you will have individual and team training plans and there will be a system within which to implement these. The prioritising that you have done will provide you with a timetable for moving forward. You will now need to consider how you are going to meet your requirements in terms of training and development opportunities.

Some people will require attendance at formal courses. This will probably form the backbone of a much wider initiative involving other solutions – and will also be the most constrained according to what financial resources you have available.

Other Initiatives to Consider

In the case study exercises which led to the development of this book, several imaginative initiatives were discovered in relation to staff training needs which did not necessarily require extensive changes or large injections of cash.

These included

- Job rotation: moving staff around the building to different departments;
- Having short regular in-house training periods, e.g. 09:00 – 09:30 before visitors enter; the skills being taught have included updating on security, lifting and handling, telephone skills and language skills (making the French/German visitor welcome at reception);
- Updating courses for attendants on new exhibits or new information on an existing one;
- A recruitment leaflet targeted at volunteers detailing in which areas of the museum's work volunteers could assist, and illustrating what would be expected of any volunteer.
- Coaching and mentoring, shadowing a colleague, being seconded to another section or another museum. Thus, the role of the experienced member of staff, whether curatorial or attendant also includes coaching. This can add an enrichment to the role of the coach and provide useful training for the other staff.
- The creation of a 'learning environment' within the museum, so that staff get used to learning from each other. For instance, adopting the

practice of asking staff who have been on courses to report back to colleagues. This reporting back via short informal presentations and/ or brief written reports not only enables others to share ideas, but creates an expectation that training is not entirely about self-fulfilment – team and museum development becomes a recognised goal as well.

- Internal peer group discussions. Information-sharing about new exhibitions between curators who are responsible for mounting the exhibits and attendant staff who will be speaking to the public.

Activity

What imaginative initiatives have already taken place in your museum regarding training and development needs?

What initiatives could be put in place related to the needs you have now identified?

Meeting the requirements of the current TNA is only a foundation for the future of training and development provision within your museum. At this point it would be useful to consider the role of the person who has been given responsibility for training matters. It is this person who can co-ordinate your new approach to staff development and training and make sure that the results of the TNA are implemented coherently throughout the museum. They should also have a long-term view of development, ensuring that there is a commitment to repeating the TNA exercise (at least in part) on a regular basis.

Whilst a TNA will provide you with information about the current situation, this will need to be updated within the next year and thereafter. Rather than trying to make extra work, it is advisable to include this process in some other regular review system, whether this takes the form of appraisal, career review or performance management. If, however, this type of review does not occur in your museum (as suggested in the checklist on p. 31), then training needs will have to be seen as a separate entity and should be updated on a formal and regular basis at least annually, for each member of staff.

In addition, for any development to have its maximum impact, staff should be encouraged to share any new skills or knowledge that they acquire with others and an evaluation strategy should form part of the training manager's plans.

Simple evaluation forms that provide information about the value of a course/developmental experience can be used.

The information collected not only outlines the value of the input to the individual, but it can also make people think how their development benefits the museum as a whole. In addition, it serves as a form of 'quality control', since the merit of the experience will be judged by the participant and issues such as value for money and applicability can be monitored. Sample pre-training and post-training activity questionnaires are included in the Tool Kit.

Conclusion

The book has taken you through all the stages of preparing to think and plan strategically for training and developing your staff as well as providing you with the methodology to undertake a full TNA. The Tool Kit which follows provides you with the tools that you need in order to carry out the work that is required.

Activity
Take one last look at what you have learnt so far. List any items that you need to go back over or learn more about, before getting on with the planning and implementation of your future development strategy and TNA.

The Tool Kit

Contents

i.   A Museum Training and Development Policy

Introduction

A training and development policy is a statement of the museum's commitment to staff training and development and a broad indication of the mechanisms by which the needs for individuals are to be assessed and met. The policy should define the relationship of the museum's commitment to training with the planning of its services as a whole.

A training policy not only provides guidelines to museum managers but also provides information for its staff. It provides a framework in which decisions can be made about what training and development activity is carried out in any given year.

It is important that the policy is developed by the museum in a way which reflects, among other things, the nature of the service the museum provides, the range and skill mix of staff involved, the size of the museum and the particular developments which face it in the foreseeable future.

Consequently, a policy reflects the particular position of a given museum at a certain stage in its development and is itself subject to review from time to time in the light of changes which will occur.

Nevertheless, it is possible to offer guidance on the form such a policy might take which can help those with the task of preparing one. It is perhaps important to stress that if at present you do not have a written policy, the process of commitment to paper is a valuable activity which should capture the current unwritten policy and not be a statement of unrealistic and potentially unrealisable activities. It should be a broad, simple and clear communication about the museum's position and intentions about the training and development of staff.

Key Areas to Include

A general statement of the museum's commitment to the training and development of staff, e.g. 'The museum of . . . is committed to the provision of quality training and development opportunities for staff to enable the successful achievement of its aims and objectives, the betterment of the staff and the improvement of the service it provides to the public. The museum affirms the value of staff training and development from initial recruitment of the individual and throughout the career of the member of staff within the museum'.

A statement about those within the museum who have primary responsibility for the overall co-ordination of identifying and meeting needs.

Ideally, in larger museums one senior person should have responsibility for the co-ordination of training and development as part of his/her job (e.g. the curator), and section-managers should have devolved responsibility for the identification of their staff needs and how they may best be met. In smaller museums, it would be more appropriate to vest all these responsibilities in one person.

An indication of the framework for assessment of training and development needs to be linked to the museum's forward plan (and, if in place, a career review process), e.g. the museum will undertake a regular (annual) assessment of development needs for staff in relation to its current and future needs. This will include staff aspirations expressed in career reviews in so far as these are in line with the museum's needs.

A statement about the development of training plans, who is responsible for their creation and at what levels within the museum, e.g. managers in the museum are responsible for the development of individual and section training and development plans (on an annual basis) and these should be discussed and agreed with individuals and groups of staff. Where appropriate, training standards should be linked to nationally recognised awards such as professional and technical qualifications or Scottish/National Vocational Qualifications.

A statement about resources required to meet identified training and development plans, e.g. the resources available for training and development of staff in the museum will have to increase in order to satisfy successfully the needs identified. The museum will seek to identify the resources required through the forward planning process so that these will develop/be acquired alongside the increasing demands.

A statement about the availability of learning/development opportunities appropriate to the needs of different staff groups and the responsibility of managers and section-heads for the dissemination of information about such opportunities, e.g. through inclusion of information in regular staff meetings, circulation of training opportunities, etc.

A statement about communicating the museum's policy on training and development to all staff.

In larger museums, an indication of the ways in which the policy will be put into practice at section/departmental level.

Developments from the Policy

The development of a written and published training and development policy can lead to the creation of a procedure which outlines how the policy is to be realised in a fair and effective way for staff in the museum. This is perhaps of particular relevance in a context where perceived needs far outstrip available resources and prioritising and longer term planning are needed to ensure that training issues are addressed systematically.

Finally, it is important to consider how you can communicate the museum's commitment to training and developing staff and the benefits this produces to the public. For example, a statement of this commitment can be included in publicity material or in publications. It can be displayed at the entrance to the museum beside any other awards or certificates. (Museums which achieve the Investor in People standard can display a special plaque.)

ii.   Developing a Job Description

Introduction

Job descriptions are based on a careful analysis of the job and should be as factual as possible.

They are important in a number of ways – they provide a clear indication of what is expected of a member of staff, they form the basis of recruitment and selection, e.g. in drawing up an advertisement, and, particularly in this context, they provide the basis for assessing training needs for the individual and groups of related staff. The discipline of reviewing existing job descriptions (or creating a new one if needed) is well worth the effort as changes and developments take place.

Within a museum there are many different kinds of jobs and it is useful to adopt an approach to developing job descriptions which will incorporate the range and be flexible enough to reflect changing roles.

The following guidance is intended to provide a framework for this activity and clearly needs to be interpreted and adapted for local needs. Remember, a 'job description' is relevant as much to a volunteer as a paid member of staff.

Framework
Job details
- Job title;
- Current grade;
- Name of section/department;
- Location of post.

Purpose of the job

This should provide a concise statement in no more than about 20 words of why the job exists in the museum.

Scope of the job

This should cover information about the scope of the job in as factual a way as possible:
- Budget-holder, responsibility for cash-float and accounting for shop sales daily, staff;
- Reporting to job holder, dealing with visitors' questions, providing conservation expertise for the collections of . . . etc.

How the job fits into the museum's organisation

- Who is the 'line manager/section-head' to whom this person reports?
- Who are the main colleagues?
- Who are job holder's staff (if relevant)?

Knowledge, skills and experience required

Summaries of the main knowledge, skills, attitudes and experience required to perform the job to a competent level. If the job requires professional/technical qualifications, these should be indicated.

Key results areas

Key results areas are statements of the end results required of the job. They describe the why and the what rather than the how of the job. Ideally they give an indication of outcomes, achievements and standards rather than a list of duties and tasks. The main characteristics of key results areas are:

- they represent the key outputs of the job;
- they are worded in terms which emphasise action that leads to an end result;
- they use specific wording rather than vague statements; and
- they provide a basis for the measurement of work against standards and thus help immensely in identifying training needs.

Identifying key results areas may prove the most demanding part of drawing up a job description. However, in this form they can be reviewed more easily in the light of changes in the service provided by the museum and in discussion with existing job holders. In general terms, most jobs will have between five and ten key results areas.

Communications and working relationships

This part describes the various people within the museum (excluding the 'boss' and reporting staff if relevant) and outside, with whom the job holder needs to have contact. It also specifies the type of communication required and its purpose in relation to the activity of the museum.

Job description agreement

For existing jobs with job holders in post, it is good practice for the 'manager' to discuss and agree the job description with the job holder as an accurate, comprehensive and clear picture of the job. This will also enable discussion and identification of training and development needs to be grounded in the requirements of the job.

Sources of Information in Drawing up a Job Description

- existing job descriptions;
- current job holders;
- museum's forward plan;
- national standards;
- outside contacts;
- peer group etc.

If a vacancy arises, it is good practice to review the post and the job description with the outgoing post holder to find out what possible changes and improvements could, or should, be made.

General comments on job descriptions

National standards of competence developed for S/NVQs can be used to check, develop or construct new job descriptions. For example:

1. If you wish to check the job description, decide what you want the job to encompass and compare this with the relevant standards.

2. If you wish to develop existing job descriptions, follow the same process as in No 1 above and use the standards to indicate what could be included and see how this differs from what you already have in place.
   For example, take an assistant keeper who is developing a computerised documentation system. This particular aspect of their job was not included in the original description but can be reasonably incorporated due to changes in technology. The job description now needs to be developed in line with these changes and should take into account the new national standards, MDA guidelines, etc.

3. If you wish to construct completely new job descriptions, use these standards as the basis of what criteria you wish to include.
   Any of these processes utilising nationally agreed standards, or guidelines will assist with the identification of training needs to be undertaken in terms of the individual job holder.
   For example, if you wish to update/develop your job descriptions without starting from scratch, it is possible to use the current national standards as a basis for the criteria to include in the descriptions. Take the list of standards and extract the relevant statements.

   > e.g. For Heritage Care and Visitor Services Level 2, S/NVQ, Unit: *Control the security of items in the premises*. The first element is 'Control access to the premises'.

This could be incorporated among others in the revised job description. Reference to the good museum assistant job description provides a useful example of linking the job description to the nationally determined standard.

A good job description is of benefit to individual members of staff, a staff team as a whole and the museum itself.

It gives staff a clear picture of what they are employed to do; to whom they are responsible; how problems can be addressed; how their roles, duties or tasks relate to those of others in the organisation and it can help staff feel that they make a real contribution to the work of the museum as a whole.

A good job description is also the basis of:

- recruitment and selection of staff;
- good employee relations;
- coherent staff training and development;

and for feedback, whether through a formal review or appraisal process or more informally.

Two contrasting job descriptions are provided for the post of museum assistant – one good and one not so good. These are followed by descriptions for a curatorial post which also represents good practice in this area.

Example of a Poor Job Description: Museum Assistant

MUSEUM ASSISTANT
Duties and responsibilities

1. To undertake where necessary general duties regarding safety and security of buildings, collections and contents.
2. To be responsible for recognising and rectifying hazardous situations.
3. To deal with visitors in a way that is deemed to be appropriate.
4. To undertake cleaning and portering tasks when time permits.
5. To cover the work of others in the museum when requested.
6. To undertake any other duties that your supervisor may determine from time to time.

Responsible to
the supervisor

Hours of work – 40 per week on a shift basis to be determined by the supervisor.

Comment

The above job description fails to encompass the range and weighting of the various activities which museum assistants are now expected to undertake (refer to S/NVQ standards which are available from the Museum Training Institute or your Area Museum Council).

The detailed responsibilities are vague and imprecise and leave too much scope for individual interpretation by the supervisor *and* the job holder (and as such could lead to difficulties in cases of grievance and disciplinary procedures).

It would be difficult to identify the person specification requirements from this type of job description (see note on person specification on pp. 103-104).

Appraisal and evaluation of performance would be difficult to undertake based on such a vague description of duties.

Such a job description would not enable the easy identification of training and staff development needs in terms of both the supervisor or the job holder.

Compare this with the job description which follows.

Example of a Good Job Description: Museum Assistant

JOB TITLE MUSEUM ASSISTANT

Department Department of Cultural Services, Museums and Galleries Division

Job purpose To maintain the safety and security of buildings and collections and provide assistance to the public.

Major tasks

Maintain the safety and security of buildings and collections	55%
Assist the public	10%
Carry out sales and reception duties	15%
Carry out ancillary duties such as cleaning, portering, basic maintenance, etc.	20%

Organisational chart

Security Services Manager
↓
Assistant Security Services Manager
↓
Museum Assistant (4 Full-time, 2 Part-time)

Job activities
Maintain the safety and security of buildings and collections
- Open and close buildings and act as keyholder. Set building security systems.
- Patrol public areas of buildings during opening hours as directed.
- Monitor security and fire alarm systems and test regularly, according to procedures. Set and monitor security alarms for individual displays or exhibits.
- Ensure familiarity with individual building layouts and accident and emergency procedures.
- Take an active part in emergency evacuations, ensuring the safety of the public and security of collections. Record incidents as appropriate.
- Ensure familiarity with safety equipment in individual buildings, e.g. type and location of fire extinguishers.
- Monitor building environment for health and safety hazards, e.g. unsafe condition of floor surfaces. Report to management and record incidents.
- Monitor the operation of environmental control equipment and carry out regular maintenance as required.
- Monitor public and private areas of buildings. Check identity passes and challenge unauthorised access. Monitor visitors for inappropriate and suspicious behaviour. Notify external agencies and management, and record incidents.
- Book business visitors in and out of building and issue and return keys.
- Supervise contractors on-site.
- Carry out standby or nightshift duties as required.

Assist the public
- Ensure familiarity with exhibits and special events in the building and answer general queries from the public. Refer more complex queries to the appropriate curatorial staff.
- Give exhibit demonstrations as appropriate.
- Have a working knowledge of what is on offer at the Local Authority's museums and galleries and advise the public. Give general assistance to visitors, e.g. refer to Tourist Information Centre for accommodation.
- Check signs and notices on display and ensure they are up to date.
- Accept complaints and suggestions from the public. Complete related paperwork.
- Assist members of the public in the event of accident. Contact the trained First Aider and emergency services if appropriate.

Carry out sales and reception duties
- Carry out sales and reception duties at any point in the division as required.
- Deal with inquiries by the public in person, by telephone or by post.
- Serve customers at the sales counter.
- Follow appropriate financial procedures, e.g. prepare cash for banking, maintain stock records.

Carry out ancillary duties
- Carry out cleaning duties inside and outside the building.
- Carry out portering duties, including moving exhibits and furnishings, often of high value or potentially fragile.
- Assist at special functions and events.
- Undertake basic maintenance work, e.g. change light bulbs.
- Deliver goods and messages and drive the museum van.

Analysis of performance requirements
Supervisory and managerial responsibility
- None

Decisions made
- The Museum Assistant has agreed procedures to follow with regard to emergencies, health and safety hazards, suspicious incidents. However, the post holder must decide him/herself when it is appropriate to take action.

Supervision received
- The Museum Assistant will carry out duties with little direct supervision, as line management will not always be present in the building, but will be in regular contact. Problems can be taken to museum management as they arise.

Work complexity
- The post holder must have detailed knowledge about emergency and security procedures in each of the buildings in the division, as well as being able to advise the public about local exhibits in some detail. Must be familiar with items on display in area to be patrolled. Must know about stock carried and financial procedures to follow when working in the shop.

Special conditions
- None

Contacts

- Contact with museum management receiving information on exhibitions, and notifying security and other problems. Continuous contact with the public supervising behaviour, giving information and working in the shop.

Creative work

- The post holder must be able to complete accurate paperwork on incidents, and carry out financial recording procedures and stock control in museum shops.

Education

- The post holder must have the ability to carry out financial procedures and complete a range of paperwork.

Experience

- Sufficient experience to supervise the public and deal appropriately with a range of situations, ranging from accidents to attempted theft.

Additional information

- As the post holder will have access to items of high value and/or knowledge of security systems, she/he is required to be of good character.
- For that reason this post has been designated as sensitive by the Local Authority and, as such, applicants are required to disclose unspent convictions (in accordance with the Rehabilitation of Offenders Act, 1974).
- The post is subject to the Performance Assessment Agreement for Museum Assistants and the post holder will be required to participate in training and development activities as part of this agreement
- This is a uniformed post. Staff must wear the uniform provided (jacket and skirt or trousers) at all times when on duty in public areas. Staff are responsible for keeping the uniform in good condition. Uniform should be worn with light coloured shirt (with tie) or blouse and dark coloured formal shoes. In appropriate conditions the jacket may be removed with the Supervisor's consent.
- Staff are expected to behave at all times in a courteous manner to the public and fellow members of staff.

Comment

The second job description for a Museum Assistant encompasses all of the areas covered in 'Developing a Job Description'.

The detail provided under each heading gives a clear outline of what the job is, how it fits into the current organisational structure and the responsibilities and expectations attached to the post.

Anyone reading the description would gain a clear picture of the job and know whether they were appropriate for the role or not.

The breakdown of tasks and expectations would allow deficits (and therefore training opportunities) in the applicant's/post holder's experience to be easily identified.

The use of the terms 'as required', and 'as appropriate' are used in some areas to indicate an element of discretion where the post holder will be expected to carry out a duty within specified procedures, e.g. 'record incidents as appropriate'. The term 'as directed' is used sometimes as an indication of the limits of the discretionary aspects of the post, e.g. patrol public areas . . . as directed' – something which would be determined by the supervisor.

Example of a Job Description: Keeper of Fine Art

JOB TITLE   KEEPER OF FINE ART

Department Department of Museums and Galleries

Job purpose Manage a specialist section in accordance with the aims and objectives of the department.

Major tasks Contribute to the management of the department 10%
Organise the work of the section   35%
Carry out tasks related to the work of the section 45%
Assist with the work of other sections   10%

Organisation detail of the museum's structure and policies
(to be inserted)

Job activities
- Contribute to the management of the department
- Participate in the work of the departmental management team
- Represent the department at meetings within the department, the Council or with outside bodies.
- Assist with the formulation of policies (e.g. collection/disposal).
- Convene section and building meetings to convey information to/ from staff.
- Prepare specialist reports for departmental management team, Cultural Services Committee, etc.
- Lead or participate in, multi-disciplinary project groups.
- Carry out specific department-wide tasks.
- Assist with the management of major projects.

Organise the work of the section

- Agree sectional work targets with the Director/Assistant Director.
- Allocate work to staff within the section.
- Identify and allocate work in addition to targets.
- Participate in the recruitment, selection, training and supervision of staff.
- Manage delegated budgets.
- Ensure the provision of resources, equipment, etc. needed for the effective execution of the work of the section.
- Accept donations which fall within the collection policy, purchase items up to a value specified by the Assistant Director and make recommendations for purchases over that value.
- Manage the museum on a day to day basis, liaising with appropriate staff within the department and elsewhere.
- Carry out joint projects with other sections/divisions/outside agencies.

Carry out tasks related to the work of the section

- Undertake documentation of the collections: identification; classification; cataloguing; indexing.
- Create/assist with temporary exhibitions on themes related to the work of the section.
- Research and create permanent displays.
- Carry out research projects.
- Answer public inquiries by letter, phone or in person.
- Give talks/lectures to outside organisations at all levels (professional, academic, community, school).

Analysis of performance requirements

Supervisory and managerial responsibility

Depute Keeper, two Assistant Keepers.   AP Grade V.

Decisions made

- Allocation of work to staff according to their knowledge and abilities: prioritisation of work within section; minor expenditure; acceptance of donations to collections; purchase of specimens of low value; identification of objects and their component materials (often reliant on experience and knowledge as opposed to basic reference books); classification of objects; selection of staff (in collaboration with colleagues and in accordance with procedures); suitability of projects for community groups etc. (judgement).

Supervision received

- Broad guidelines set by Assistant Director: mutually agreed targets: plans own work and that of section subject to seeking occasional guidance from Assistant Director. Works within policies laid down.

Work complexity

- Must be professionally skilled and able to supervise/organise staff. Work includes outside organisations as well as working within department. Wide range of activities (e.g. working with collections, working with people, working creatively).

Special conditions

- None

Contacts

- Apply professional skill and judgment in advising/seeking assistance from officials at all levels within the Council. Work with community groups, etc. to foster their self-awareness, self-belief. Also contacts with professional colleagues elsewhere at all levels.

Creative work

- Devise programmes of activities, exhibitions, displays. Research and write text for publications and museum displays. Write reports for departmental management team and committee. Interpretation and presentation of complex information. Creation/adaptation of specialist classification/object systems.

Educational/vocational qualifications

- Degree in relevant discipline; Associateship of the Museums Association (AMA) or Level 4 S/NVQ. The post holder will be expected to keep abreast of current changes in professional practice and undertake Continuing Professional Development.

Minimum experience required

- Between three and five years experience of museum work in the appropriate field.

Additional Information

- The job has important security considerations so staff must be of good character.

iii. Compiling a Person Specification

When you have examined the job description carefully then it is helpful to think about any expertise, experience and personal qualities or characteristics which you feel the individual who is to occupy the job might need. This is called the **person specification**. This is a way of helping you when either selecting candidates for a new post, replacing someone in an existing post, or when considering clarifying or resetting a role for an existing staff member. The person specification can be particularly useful in helping to select candidates for interview, as you can score applicants according to how well they match the person specification. In addition, it can be used to draw up appropriate questions when the time comes to interview those selected.

These categories are not intended to be a set format, simply guides.

Physical Considerations

Are there any aspects about the job in which, apart from 'normal health', there should be any qualification in terms of being able to work under particular conditions?

Are there any adaptations that could be used to make it more possible to employ a person with a disability?

Education and Training

Are there any particular requirements here – vocational certificates, professional qualifications, etc.? Requirements change and are changing rapidly. It is important to keep up to date and to be aware of equivalencies between 'old' and 'new' qualifications.

Experience

Does this need to be directly relevant or could similar kinds of experience in a different environment be considered (might it be in some cases an advantage)? There are various points here – the length of time spent doing a job may not always be so important as range and variety of experience.

Specialist Skills and Knowledge

This is the kind of specialist ability without which the job cannot be done, for instance technical or computing skills. The difficult question is how does one assess such skills at interview? If you are looking at internal candidates, the question may be, how quickly can this person be trained to a satisfactory level.

Drive and Motivation

When recruiting someone new, it is useful also to consider why a person might wish to do the job.

Personality and Disposition

This is a very difficult area. You may say that you are looking for someone for the reception post who is 'outgoing, friendly and gets on with people'. The difficulty is measuring these traits. If you are using existing staff, a redeployment for instance, then it is quite possible that you and others in a supervisory position will have formed some impressions. However, some people may not show their personality if managed in a particular way, and their outgoing friendliness may not blossom.

If selecting someone new then this is an area most difficult to assess and most prone to bias at interview.

Special Circumstances

This only forms part of the person specification where it is relevant to the job, e.g. staying away from home, working weekends. Great care must be exercised when asking these questions at interviews otherwise overt discrimination may occur if they appear to be about the **person** and not the **particular job** in question.

References

If possible, references should be available to the interviewers but it is not uncommon to offer the post subject to the receipt of satisfactory references. Care should be exercised, however, as job applicants rarely cite referees who will give an unsatisfactory reference.

Remember, the starting point for developing the person specification is the job description.

iv.   Checklist for TNA Interviews

Do you have trained interviewers?

⬇

What can you do to improve interviewing skills?

⬇

Should people be interviewed alone or in a small group?

⬇

When and where is the best time to see people?

⬇

Everyone must be asked the same questions

⬇

Have a room set aside if possible that is not dark/cold/noisy, etc.

⬇

Set a time-scale for the interview

⬇

Explain the purpose of the interview

⬇

Always give people time to answer the questions

⬇

Do not ask leading questions

⬇

Record the responses given accurately

⬇

Explain that the responses will be used as part of a report and not in a detrimental way for the individual

v.   Conducting TNA Interviews

Make an appointment at a time suitable to both you and the interviewee

↓

Find an appropriate space for the interview

↓

Set a time-scale for the interview and stick to it, e.g. half an hour or an hour

↓

Explain the purpose of the interview, how the interviewee(s) have been chosen to take part and what will happen to the information that they give

↓

Ask the questions as they are set out in the schedule. Always ask each interviewee all the questions – let them decide if they are relevant or not

↓

Prompt the interviewee if he/she does not understand the question by either repeating it or rephrasing it

↓

Do not rush the interviewee

↓

Communication – the way you treat people affects how they respond to you, so look relaxed and interested, and listen attentively

↓

Do not put words into their mouth if they are having difficulty responding

↓

Record what they are saying fully, accurately and legibly

↓

At the end of the interview give them a chance to add any other comments that they might wish to make or to ask questions if they wish to

↓

Let the interviewee know what the time-scale is for analysing the information and producing the results so that he/she can look out for the report and its outcomes

vi.   Designing TNA Questionnaires

Does anyone in-house have expertise in designing questionnaires?

↓

What can you do to develop or improve the relevant skills?

↓

Always pilot a questionnaire before using it

↓

Do not ask leading questions

↓

Use a combination of open and closed questions

↓

Design the form with ease of analysis in mind – do not make it too long or complicated

↓

Only ask one thing at a time in each question

↓

Each individual should receive their own questionnaire

↓

Always set a time-scale for the return of the form – usually 10–14 days

↓

Give clear instructions about how to complete the form

↓

Let people know where to return the form to, in confidence

vii.   Pro-forma Individual TNA Interview Questionnaire

1. Please describe your present post (title/grade/description/full/ part time/volunteer).

2. Please indicate briefly how you spend your time in the post, i.e. your key duties.

3. How long have you been in your current post? (years, months).

4. What a) qualifications b) training did you need for this particular post?

   a.

   b.

5. Please list the skills, knowledge and experience that you feel are necessary to do your job effectively.

6a. Please describe any training that you have received since you joined this museum.

6b. What, if any, of this training have you received whilst in your current post?

6c. Has this training been adequate in terms of your current needs, and if not, then what training would you like to have received/would have been useful?

7. At present, how do you hear about courses or other training opportunities?

8. How do you apply for any of these courses or training opportunities, i.e. who do you ask, or who asks you if you would like to go?

9. What changes/developments do you see in your current job over the next three years for which you think you may require further specialist or specialist training?

10. Looking even further ahead, what changes do you foresee in your museum? Say briefly how such changes might influence the way you do your job and any training that you think might be required in order to help you cope with the changes. (NB for the manager this also includes a strategic view for the whole museum.)

11. Given the option, what form/s of training would you prefer? (Please circle those which you would prefer – you may choose a combination of these.)

Within the museum/day-release/exchange with another museum/correspondence course/courses organised by Area Museum Council/short 1 – 3-day courses/longer courses organised by external trainers/courses organised by Universities, Local Authority etc.

Other, please specify

12. What further training (if any) whether specialised or general, do you feel you could now benefit from in order to perform your current job to your satisfaction?

13. If chargehand or supervisor of department, then ask: what training would you like to see the staff in your department receive? Are there any particular areas of difficulty that you think could usefully be addressed?

14. What training do you think your managers and those people that you work with (where applicable) would benefit from?

15. Please feel free to make any other comments on training that you would like to be considered in the report.

Thank you for your help.

viii. Pro-forma Manager/Assistant Manager Interview Questionnaire

1. Thinking about staff performance and any particular problems you can identify, please describe how you could see any deficits being met by training or further experience?

    _____

    _____

    _____

2. In order to put together an 'environmental map' of how you see future influences on the museum, describe what factors you think are relevant to the following areas:

    Legal _____

    Financial _____

    Educational/Social _____

    Technological _____

    Professional _____

    Ethical _____

    Demographic _____

    Political _____

3. Can you describe how you would like to see training being located, planned and provided for, i.e. the museum in the future?

    _____

    _____

    _____

Thank you for your help.

112

ix.   Guidelines for Using a Team Training Log

To be completed by Section Manager/Supervisor

Notes for Use

Thank you for agreeing to complete this log in the context of the TNA. We hope that the following notes will be useful in explaining what we would like you to do.

What is the Analysis?

It is a survey of the current state of training provision within the museum and particularly how this affects you and those working with you in their ability to carry out the work to your satisfaction.

It also focuses on future training needs based on your experience of working with your 'team'.

What is Your Role?

To record situations that you come across at work where you feel the knowledge, skills and experience of your team (rather than yourself) are not adequate to meet the demands that are being made on them. Through this, potential learning situations can be highlighted and training needs targeted.

How is this Done?

By making a record over the next five days as and when you feel there is a gap between how your team (individually or when working together) do the job and how you would like them to be able to perform it. For example:

- How they assemble an exhibit and how you would like them to do so.
- How they deal with a visiting school party and how you would like them to do so.

We have provided a pro-forma (see p. 115) which you can use for your observations, but please do not feel obliged to fill it all in. Record as much or as little as you feel is appropriate. Do try and write things down as soon as possible after the event as it is easy to forget the details after even a short period of time. Whether you have written anything or not, please stop and think back every two hours about what has happened to you at work and catch up on anything that you have not had time to record yet. In this way, nothing should get lost.

When you have completed the recording, please sign and return the forms to

---

All the information that you provide will be confidential and your name will not be revealed in the report.

Thank you for your help.

x.   Pro-forma Team Training Log

Sheet for Supervisor/Manager's Observations

Museum _____

Post _____

Situation/Activity	What knowledge/skills would have helped your team?

xi. Guidelines for Compiling a Training Plan for the Team

The team log will help you identify the kind of training you as a team may require.

We all too often think that training is about an individual and his or her own development. However, as most staff in museums work in teams we must consider the importance of teams and training.

Thinking of training for a team is a useful exercise. It can provide valuable insights into respective roles and how individual needs relate to those of the team. It can also point to potential gaps and problem areas for the team that looking through a series of individual training needs might not reveal.

For example, consider a group of attendants. Each one will have some training needs in such matters as knowledge of security systems, alarms, etc. Because they share shifts together, however, and are **collectively** responsible for security throughout the museum, it would be a very useful exercise for them to sit down as a team, with or without their supervisor or line manger, and ask themselves the following questions.

Although we are all involved in security, when it comes to an emergency who does what, in what order and with what equipment?

What would happen if an emergency occurred and only two out of the three were on duty (the other member being ill or at lunch)? Would this mean that we would need some extra training in how to make an effective response?

We can give quite precise ideas as to the required training needed to fill these gaps.

A great deal of work in any museum is based upon **team responsibility**. Teams work best when there is a clear identification of both individual and team roles and responsibilities. This is true whether one considers volunteers, keepers, attendants, technicians or sales staff.

The completion of a team training log can not only help in the identification of such needs but contribute towards the development of a team 'ethos' which is **positive to training and development.** There are some particular issues:

- As training budgets are limited then who in the team should receive training? Do we have a fair and sensible method for making this decision, or is it a matter of 'it's your turn' or seniors first?

- If only one in the team is selected to go for training then how can we all gain from it, i.e. what systems have we got to cascade the information and skills to all the team? If we do have a system, can we improve it?

We have already mentioned the importance of coaching. This is exactly the situation where some form of coaching can be very necessary: where one member of the team has received some training and other members need to share this.

Coaching on a one-to-one or one-to-small-group basis is often much better than asking a member of the group to stand up and give a presentation. This can create very real stress and in some cases even put members of staff off ever going on a training course because of the 'horror show' that awaits them back at work.

- Increasingly teams may have to examine their skill/talent mix, e.g. language skills for reception/shop staff. Who has already got a smattering of French and who could be put in for a Spanish course? Which particular skill do we need and we do not have, or have only in part? Skills mix means that not everyone has to have the same range of skills – we do, however, need a mix to create a team, a mix of personalities, talents and roles.

Remember, in compiling a team training plan enter each person's name and then against the descriptions of needs, e.g. customer care, professional update, security training etc, place a comment if the person needs that type of input and assess its urgency.

xii. Guidelines for using a Training Log for the Individual

Notes for Use

Thank you for agreeing to complete this log. We hope that the following notes will be useful in explaining what we would like you to do.

What is the Survey?

It concerns the current state of training provision within the museum and particularly how this affects you and your ability to carry out your work to your satisfaction. It also seeks to look at what future training needs might be, based on the experience of staff and the direction of future plans for your museum.

What is Your Role?

It is to record any situations you come across at work where you feel that the knowledge, skills and experience that you have are not adequate to meet the demands that are being made on you. In this way potential learning situations are highlighted and any training needs can be assessed.

How is this Done?

You are asked to make a record over the next five days as and when you feel there is a gap between how you can do the job now and how you would like to be able to do the job. These situations could be anything from a highly technical or specialist knowledge issue, to not knowing how to deal with a visitor to the museum who poses a specific problem.

We have provided a pro-forma which you can use for your observations, but please do not feel obliged to fill it all in. Record as much or as little as you feel is appropriate. Do try and write things down as soon as possible after the event as it is easy to forget the details after even a short period of time. Whether you have written anything or not, please stop and think back every two hours about what has happened to you at work and catch up on anything that you have not had time to record yet. In this way, nothing should get lost.

When you have completed the recording, please sign and return the forms to

All the information that you provide will be confidential and your name will not be revealed in the report.

Thank you for your help.

xiii. Pro-forma Individual Training Log

Sheet for Recorder's Observations

Museum _____

Post _____

Situation/Activity	What knowledge/skills would have helped your team?

xiv. Guidelines for Compiling a Training Plan for the Individual

The important point to begin with is, what does this member of staff do now?

You need to know this in order to draw a **baseline**.

You may think we know what the person does by the title he or she carries or from previous encounters with the job holder. It may be, however, that this person actually carries out the job in quite a novel way. Perhaps it is done in a way that actually shortcuts normal procedures, or performed according to all the procedures but still in such a way that causes difficulties to that person or more likely to his or her colleagues and visitors. In other words there may be a training need.

How do you find out what the member of staff actually does? It is not so obvious as it may first appear.

By Asking

'What do you do?' may get you only a partial answer. The staff member may well try to accentuate the role in a way that he or she might think will please/satisfy or interest the questioner. This is particularly likely if the questioner happens to be the person's manager. Think how you might answer that particular question if someone asked you. The more complex the job, the more difficult it is to explain it to someone else.

By Observing

There are difficulties here which are accentuated if this is done by a line manager. One way round this is to make use of someone from outside that specific department, but naturally this has to be handled very carefully. It must be put into a positive light: 'I'd like X to join you for a morning so that you can both do some thinking on the kind of tasks you do and the way you do them, then we can see if any training might be necessary'. Such observation is not meant to be an inspection or a time and motion study. It must be seen as a genuine attempt to assist staff with the identification of their training needs.

By Reading

Consulting records and referring to a job description. Remember that any such description may be out of date, may not be very comprehensive and may not show any priority or weighting in terms of tasks to be done and amount of the staff member's time to be spent in any one area. Remember too, that priorities change within a job description and that these changes may not have been registered.

By Making Use of an Appraisal Scheme

This can, assuming there is a degree of trust in the system, point to directions where there may be a training deficit. An appraisal is not by itself a training audit, it takes on board a great deal more than that. In any appraisal, however, there should be a question or number of direct questions which relate to training, such as:

Given your present job description are there any areas in which you feel that you require training?

There may also be some more **indirect** ones which will lead to consideration of various training needs:

What parts of your job do you enjoy doing and what parts do you feel less happy with?

As mentioned elsewhere in this book it is very important in any appraisal to make sure that training is not seen as the only answer to a particular shortcoming and, that any promises made in the appraisal which relate to training, are adhered to.

Increasingly organisations are using the concept of key results areas 'KRAS', (see p. 93 on developing a Job Description) to assist them with job performance and appraisal. This means that the general job description may be broken down into key areas and any appraisal interview will focus very much on how the individual carried these out in the period under review.

Whatever system or combination of systems are used to identify training needs you then have to move to the establishment of a **training plan**.

It is vital that there should be **clarification** of what exactly is meant by the term training. Training can, and should, mean much more than attending courses and being provided with instruction. It is very important to make it known that training can be a range of possibilities, from one-to-one tuition, coaching, to Open University courses.

You then have to move towards a **training contract**.

The development of a training contract is one means by which to ensure that both sides are committed to the process. It is a negotiation in which both sides should win.

It is a question of . . . if you do this, then we will see that the museum does . . .

One of the lessons that can be drawn from looking at existing appraisal systems is that managers should resist the temptation to offer training and then back-track when the budgets are looked at more closely. This only breeds disappointment and cynicism in the whole appraisal/staff development process.

'Under-promise and over-achieve', might be the watch-words when it comes to the drawing up of such training contracts. Do not be tempted to rush into something extravagant: take it stage by stage. Such a contract might looks like this:

Mr X: Post Receptionist/shop attendant at (Museum)

Training Contract

Estimated cost for both objectives £

Date

Supervisor

Objective 1	Period	Training method	How assessed
Simple welcome for French visitors	Start 1st Sept Complete 1st Dec	Tapes & manual 2 hours tuition per week	French Tutor using role play

Objective 2	Period	Training method	How assessed
More extended welcome and introduction to museum for French German speaking visitors	Start 5th Jan Complete 15th May	Tapes & manual Tuition at local FE College	French tutor bringing a party of French visitors who will be in the town in July and observing interaction and completing checklist agreed with Mr X, supervisor and tutor

---

There are several points to note here. Firstly, the training objectives are **graded,** secondly the contract specifies **time periods** for completion. It is most important that these should be respected. It is so easy for time schedules to slip and if that happens a great deal of enthusiasm and commitment may also disappear.

If the training involves a skill that is not shared by both parties to the contract then some kind of **independent and expert view** should be sought on the feasibility of the time period indicated. In the example above, assuming neither side spoke French, then it would not be very sensible for them to agree on possible dates for the completion of the learning objective. They need to consult – in this case the French speaking tutor.

It is vital that there should be some agreement as to how any training will be **assessed.** Vagueness at this point will cause trouble later. Again, it may be useful to bring in outside help on this. In many cases the assessment is obvious; an exam or assessment will be taken such as an S/NVQ unit, or there will be a demonstration of whether the person can actually perform this or that task. There may be various ways of performing a set task and some kind of independent benchmark should be agreed upon.

A learning contract should also set out what **method** will be followed and provide some indication of the materials, both technical and human, that will be provided. It is useful to indicate **costings**, as this will assist in budgeting.

xv. Pro-forma Training Needs Summary Form

Name of Staff Member:

Review Date:

Training Needs	Essential	Date Completed	Preferred	Date Completed	Optional	Date Completed	Comments

xv. Pro-forma Training Needs Summary Form: Museum Assistant

Name of Staff Member:

Review Date:

Training Needs	Essential	Date Completed	Preferred	Date Completed	Optional	Date Completed	Comments
Security							
Emergency procedures update							
Fire procedures update							
Safety procedures update							
Disability awareness							
Knowledge of tills and phones							
Customer care procedures							
Foreign language phrases							
Information about displays							
Handling groups							
Lifting and handling update							
Team building							

xiv. S/NVQ Self-Assessment Checklist

An example follows where the individual has been asked to assess him/herself against the performance criteria related to some elements of competence on the following basis:

1 = I am competent and can produce evidence to prove this.
2 = I am competent but unsure regarding producing evidence of this.
3 = I am not yet competent in this area.

Element B2.2 Develop Documentation Rules

		Enter Number	Supervisor's Verification (Please Initial)
Performance Criteria:			
(a)	Structure of records meets the requirements of users and complies with relevant standards	2	
(b)	Indexing procedures are suitable to the type and size of the collection	3	
(c)	Individuals authorised to record the collection are specified	1	
(d)	The period between entry and accessioning is minimised	2	
(e)	Information that is mandatory is specified	2	
(f)	Information which is confidential is identified and access restrictions are specified	1	
(g)	Procedures for the security of the information are established	1	
(h)	Problems with the documentation rules are identified and improvements implemented	1	
(i)	Documentation rules are clearly recorded and distributed to all appropriate people	1	

Range Statements:

i) Records: manual, computerised
ii) Indexing: manual computerised
iii) Systems and equipment: manual, local area computer networks

Underpinning Knowledge:

2   Information Systems and Procedures
5   Legislation, regulations, codes of conduct and professional ethics
8   Security and protection of items and collections
12 Users and their requirements.

xvii. Pro-forma Pre-training and Development Activity Questionnaire

To be completed by training participant

Training and development activity title/description

Date(s) _____

Venue _____

Name _____

1. **Insert the objectives of the activity here (e.g. if attending a course these should be available from the course provider and are usually sent with the joining instructions).**

   e.g.

   – to encourage more effective time management.
   – to examine time management techniques and good practice.

2. **List below up to 3 specific things which you personally hope to do, or do better, as a result of this training and development activity.**

(i) _____

(ii) _____

(iii) _____

3. **Now pass this questionnaire to your line manager and discuss with him/her.**

To be completed by the Line Manager

4. List below up to 3 specific things you hope your member of staff will be able to do better as a result of this training and development activity.

(i) _____

(ii) _____

(iii) _____

I have discussed with _____ what we hope he/she will get out of this training and development activity and how the lessons learnt might be applied on return.

*Signed*_____ *Date* _____

Please return this to your member of staff, and ask them to give it to the person with responsibility for staff training and development within the museum to arrive no later than _____

Thank you both for taking the time to complete this questionnaire.

xviii. Pro-forma Post-training and Development Activity Questionnaire

Training and development activity title/description

Date(s) _____

Venue _____

Name _____

Participant and line manager to discuss and complete questionnaire approximately 3 months after the training and development activity.

1. As a result of attending this training and development activity what improvements/changes have there been to your work performance?

2. How has your section/museum benefited from these improvements/changes?

3. Looking back on the training and development activity what has been most useful?

Have you met any difficulties from the following in applying this learning?

a.	Line management	e.	Lack of follow-up help
b.	Support staff	f.	Lack of resources
c.	Pressure of work	g.	Other, please specify
d.	Nature of work		

(Circle all the difficulties you have met)

If 'e' is circled in question 4, please specify the follow-up advice or assistance that would help you.

If you completed a personal action plan as part of this training and development activity, how successful have you been in achieving it and why?

Please give this to the person with responsibility for staff training and development within the museum to arrive no later than

_____

Thank you both for taking the time to complete this questionnaire.

xix.   Selecting an External Training Provider

Once you have identified a training and development need for your museum, you might find it useful to consider the following questions before you select an external training provider to deliver this.

- When do you want the training to take place?
- Does it need to take place at the museum or 'off-the-job'?
- Could you or someone else within the museum train the member of staff yourself?
- Could the individual staff member shadow a work colleague for an agreed period instead?
- Could you make use of an open learning training package (e.g. Open College)?
- Could the learning be achieved through undertaking a placement at another museum?

The answer to these last four questions can vary considerably according to the person's experience, responsibilities and preferred learning style, e.g. open learning does not suit everyone.

- How long can you allow for the training activity (staff cover etc.)?
- How much can you invest in this training?
- What grants are available to assist with this?
- Do you want the training to be tied to an external qualification?, i.e. can the staff member be assessed at the end in order to obtain an S/NVQ unit?

Once you have decided on the above and you have obtained the details of some training providers (e.g. your local college) you might find it useful to obtain the following information from them in order to compare and select the one best suited to your needs.

- Is the training provider willing to meet you (without charge) to negotiate what you require?
- Is the training provider able to provide details of previous clients? If so, follow these up.
- Will the training be tailored to your specific needs, or is it a standard 'off-the-shelf' package?

- Has the training provider asked you about the experience level of the learners?
- What are the programme details?
- What pre-course information is available for staff?
- Who will actually deliver the training?
- What experience has the trainer had of working with museums and galleries?
- Does the training lead to a recognised qualification?
- What price will the trainer charge? Is VAT inclusive? Does it include all of the trainer's expenses?
- If the training is being delivered out of the museum, is lunch included?
- If funds permit, how would the trainer follow-up the training?
- After the training, will the trainer evaluate it with you and your staff?
- How will the trainer measure whether or not it succeeded?

Once you have talked to the training provider, consider these questions.

- Was the information you asked for given promptly and without fuss?
- Did the trainer listen to you?
- What questions did the trainer ask about the museum and the potential trainees?
- Do you think that your staff would like this trainer?
- Can you see yourself developing a working relationship over time?

Sources and Resources

Useful Contacts

Area Museum Council for the South West, Hestercombe House, Cheddon Fitzpaine, Taunton TA2 8LQ. Tel 01823-259696. Fax 01823-413114.

Arts Council of England, 14 Great Peter Street, London SW1P 3NQ. Tel 0171-333 0100. Fax 0171-973 6590.

Arts Council of Northern Ireland, 185 Stranmillis Road, Belfast BT9 5DU. Tel 01232-381591. Fax 01232-661715.

Arts Council of Wales, 9 Museum Place, Cardiff CF1 3NX. Tel 01222-394711. Fax 01222- 221447.

Association of Business Sponsorship of the Arts (ABSA), Nutmeg House, 60 Gainsford Street, Butler's Wharf, London SE1 2NY. Tel 0171-378 81443. Fax 0171-407 7527.

ABSA North, Dean Clough, Halifax HX3 5AX. Tel 01422-367860.

ABSA Northern Ireland, PO Box 496, Danesfort, 120 Malone Road, Belfast BT9 5DU. Tel 01232-664736.

ABSA Wales, 16 Museum Place, Cardiff CF1 3BH. Tel 01222-303023. Fax 01222-303024.

ABSA Scotland, 100 Wellington Street, Glasgow G2 6PB. Tel 0141-204 3864.

ABSA Midlands, Central House, Broad Street, Birmingham B1 2JP. Tel 0121-634 4104.

Association of Independent Museums (AIM), c/o London Transport Museum, 39 Wellington Street, Covent Garden, London WC2E 7BB. Tel 0171-379 6344. Fax 0171-836 4118.

Association of Leading Visitor Attractions, 4 Westminster Palace Gardens, Artillery Row, London SW1P 1RL. Tel 0171-222 1728. Fax 0171-222 1729.

Association of Scottish Visitor Attractions, Suite 6, Admiral House, 29-30 Maritime Street, Edinburgh EH6 6SE. Tel 0131-555 2551. Fax 0131-555 2552.

Convention of Scottish Local Authorities (COSLA), Rosebery House, 9 Haymarket Terrace, Edinburgh EH12 5XZ. Tel 0131-474 9200. Fax 0131-474 9292.

Council of Museums in Wales, The Courtyard, Letty Street, Cathays, Cardiff CF2 4EL. Tel 01222-225432. Fax 01222-668516.

East Midlands Museums Service, Courtyard Buildings, Wollaton Park, Nottingham NG8 2AE. Tel 0115-9854534. Fax 0115-9280038.

Industrial Society, 48 Bryanston Square, London W1H 7LN. Tel 0171-262 2401. Fax 0171-706 1096.

Industrial Society (Northern Ireland), 1st Floor, Temple Court, 41 North Street, Belfast BT1 1NA. Tel 01232-330674. Fax 01232-313631.

Industrial Society (Scotland), 3rd Floor, 4 West Regent Street, Glasgow G2 1RW. Tel 0141-332 2827. Fax 0141-332 9096.

Institute of Personnel and Development, IPD House, Camp Road, London SW19 4UX. Tel 0181-971 9000. Fax 0181-263 333. e-mail ipd@ipd.co.uk Web site http://www.ipd.co.uk

Local Government Association, 26 Chapter Street, London SW1P 4ND. Tel 0171-834 2222. Fax 1071-834 2263.

Museums Association, 42 Clerkenwell Close, London EC1R 0PA. Tel 0171-608 2933. Fax 0171-250 1929.

Museum Documentation Association, Jupiter House, Station Road, Cambridge CB1 2JD. Tel 01223-315760. Fax 01223-362521. e-mail mda@mdocassn.demon.co.uk

Museums & Galleries Commission, 16 Queen Anne's Gate, London SW1H 9AA. Tel 0171-233 4200. Fax 0171-233 3686.

Museum Training Institute, 1st Floor, Glyde House, Glydegate, Bradford BD5 0UP. Tel 01274-391056, 391087, 391092, 391773. Fax 01274-394890.

North of England Museums Service, House of Recovery, Bath Lane, Newcastle-Upon-Tyne NE4 5SQ. Tel 0191-222 1661. Fax 0191-261 4725.

Northern Ireland Museums Council, 66 Donegal Pass, Belfast BT7 1BU. Tel 01232-550215. Fax 01232-550216. e-mail museums.council@nimc.org.uk

North West Museums Service, Griffin Lodge, Cavendish Place, Blackburn BB2 2PN. Tel 01254-670211. Fax 01254-681995.

Qualifications and Curriculum Authority, 222 Euston Road, London NW1 2BZ. Tel 0171-728 1914. Fax 0171-986 579.

Scottish Arts Council, 12 Manor Place, Edinburgh EH3 7DD. Tel 0131-226 6051. Fax 0131-225 9833. e-mail sac@artsfb.org.uk

Scottish Centre for Cultural Management and Policy, Leith Campus, Duke Street, Edinburgh EH6 8HF. Tel 0131-317 3822. Fax 0131-317 3308. e-mail sccmp@leith.qmced.ac.uk

Scottish Museums Council, County House, 20-22 Torphichen Street, Edinburgh EH3 8JB. Tel 0131-229 7465. Fax 0131-229 2728. e-mail inform@scottishmuseums.org.uk

Scottish Qualifications Authority, Hanover House, 24 Douglas Street, Glasgow G2 7NQ. Tel 0141-242 2214. Fax 0141-242 2244. e-mail mail@scotvec.org.uk Web site http://www.scotvec.org.uk/SVQ

South Eastern Museums Service, Ferroners House, Barbican, London EC2Y 8AA. Tel 0171-600 0219. Fax 0171-600 2581.

West Midlands Regional Museums Council, Hanbury Road, Stoke Prior, Bromsgrove, Worcestershire B60 4AD. Tel 01527-872258. Fax 01527-576960.

Yorkshire & Humberside Museums Council, Farnley Hall, Hall Lane, Leeds LS12 5HA. Tel 0113-2638909. Fax 0113-2791479.

Further Reading

Ambrose, Timothy, *Managing new museums: a guide to good practice*. Edinburgh, HMSO, 1993.

Ambrose, Timothy M. and Runyard, Sue (eds), *Forward planning: a handbook of business, corporate and development planning for museums and galleries*. London, Museums & Galleries Commission/Routledge, 1991.

Bramley, Peter, *Evaluating training effectiveness: benchmarking your training activity*. 2nd revised edition, Maidenhead, McGraw-Hill Publishing, 1996.

Canadian Museums Association, *People, survival, change and success. Towards a human resource strategy for the future of Canadian museums*. A consultation document. Ottawa, Ontario, Canadian Museums Association, 1993.

Davies, Stuart, *Producing a forward plan. MGC Guidelines for good practice*. London, Museums & Galleries Commission, 1996.

Hackett, Penny, *Introduction to training*: London, Institute of Training and Development, 1997.

Harrison, Rosemary, *Training and Development*. London, Institute of Personnel Management, 1988.

Harrison, Rosemary, *Employee Development*. London, Institute of Training and Development, 1997.

Holloway, Anne, and Whyte, Cathy, *Mentoring: the definitive workbook*. Edited by Roy Kenning, Manchester, Development Processes (Publications), Swansea College, 1994.

Kahn, Howard, and Garden, Sally, *Job attitudes and potential stress in the museum sector*. Report of a pilot study. Sponsored by the Museum Training Institute, Bradford. Edinburgh, Heriot-Watt University of Business Organisation, 1993.

Museums & Galleries Commission, *Museum professional training and career structure*. Report of a working party 1987. London, Museums & Galleries Commission, 1987.

Museum Training Institute, *Achieving Investors in People*. A practical guide for museums, galleries and heritage organisations. Bradford, Museum Training Institute, 1996.

Museum Training Institute, *How to implement NVQs/SVQs in your organisation*. Bradford, Museum Training Institute, 1995.

Museum Training Institute, *Museum sector workforce survey: an analysis of the workforce in museum, galleries and the heritage sector in the United Kingdom*. Report prepared for MTI by the Management Centre, Bradford University, Bradford, Museum Training Institute, 1993.

Museum Training Institute, *Standards of occupational competence*. Bradford, Museum Training Institute, 1995.

FURTHER READING

Murch, Anne, *Developing and training staff in museums and galleries*. MGC Guidelines for good practice. London, Museums & Galleries Commission, 1997.

Ontario, Ministry of Citizenship and Culture, Heritage Administration Branch, *Developing a staff training policy*. Toronto, MCR.

Parsloe, Eric, *Coaching, mentoring and assessing. A practical guide to developing competence*. Revised edition, London, Kogan Page, 1995.

Reid, Margaret Anne and Barrington, Harry, *Training interventions: managing employee development*. 5th edition, London, Institute of Personnel and Development, 1997.

Siddons, Suzy, *Delivering training*. London, Institute of Personnel and Development, 1997.

Volunteer Centre UK, Publ., *Skills audit and action planner for volunteer organisation*. Berkhamstead, Volunteer Centre UK, 1991.

Index

Printed in Scotland for The Stationery Office Limited
J24009, 9/97, CCN 003808